GROWING UP
HIPPIE

Anastasia
Galadriel Machacek

Back cover Author Bio photo taken by Willow Cordain

ISBN:1477562257
ISBN-13: 978-1477562253

Cover photo taken by Gary St. Martin, 1977. To view more photos please visit: www.stmartinproductions.com

Introduction

The intention behind this book is to share my personal thoughts, experiences, and perspectives as a child growing up in the hippie era. It offers a glimpse into the life of a hippie kid raised on organic foods, New Age spiritualism, and a holistically healthy lifestyle, combined with experiences of tripping on acid and smoking pot. I wish to shed some light on the part of the '60s, '70s, and '80s that doesn't receive much attention—hippie kids. With so many young hippie parents exploring and experiencing the new ways of the hippie counterculture, one might wonder what their children experienced. Basically everything their parents did.

Most hippie kids have a unique story to tell, with pretty outrageous upbringings compared to the average kid growing up during the same era. Many may find it hard to believe that we survived the events of our radical upbringing. My childhood was filled with uncertainty: frequent moves and school changes, communal living, homelessness, travel, hitchhiking, and exposure to diverse people from all walks of life. Through my personal experiences, I have portrayed some scenarios that other hippie kids may have experienced. I realize that we all have our own interpretations of what it was like growing up as a hippie kid. There may be many parallels, some not so extreme, and others far more traumatic than my own. I can only speak for myself in regards to personal experiences and the observations of what was going on around me.

Acknowledgements

I am blessed with many friends and family members who have supported and encouraged me along the path of writing this story. First of all, I need to thank my mom, without whom I wouldn't have had such an interesting and eventful life. Elijah, my oldest son, thank you so much for letting me read excerpts of the book to you as I wrote them. Your feedback and responses were always so encouraging, and inspired me to continue. Nathaniel, my youngest son, thank you for giving me plenty of quiet space to write. Your independence and ability to entertain yourself made it possible for me to find the time to write my book. Adam, thanks for all your love and support over the past thirteen years and throughout this entire book-writing process. Much gratitude goes to my cousin Laurie, for having so much faith in me. I appreciate all of your positive feedback and encouragement to publish my story. It was an honor to have you as one of the first readers of my manuscript. Willow, Thank you for encouraging me with such enthusiasm and showing so much interest in promoting my book. Jadesong, (my BFF) you have always been an inspiration to me. I appreciate all the love and positive words you gave to me throughout this entire project. Thank you for the constructive feedback after reading my manuscript. Chris, thank you for being you. I am most grateful for your sincerity and for your encouragement to honestly share my story. Diana, thank you so much for your feedback and words of wisdom after taking on the challenge of reading my manuscript. Sage, your enthusiasm kept me inspired. I appreciate the validation and the excitement you showed when I revealed the title of the book. Alyssa, my niece, I want you to know that your opinion means the world to me, and I appreciate your eagerness to read the book. Your enthusiasm encouraged me to finish this project. Mickey Magic, I cannot tell you how I needed that extra push to be accountable for getting my book published. I appreciate your encouragement, and all the faith you have that my story will be successful. Gary St. Martin, thank you for being one of the hippies from the day who actually kept it together enough to take such amazing photos.

For Elijah and Nathaniel

Growing Up Hippie
Anastasia Galadriel Machacek

Conception

The mid-1960s and early 1970s marked the beginning of the hippie era, a time marked by radical social change. A new generation had stepped up to try to make a difference in the world and attempted to make drastic changes by challenging governmental politics and the dysfunctional ways in which they felt our society functioned. I believe that the intention was to create and inspire a universal awareness for positive change. Even though the hippie culture popped up all across the United States and spread worldwide, the heart and birthplace of the counterculture lived in the San Francisco Bay Area.

The hippie movement primarily consisted of college-aged kids looking for an alternative way to live, rebelling against the norms of mainstream culture, creating radical new ways of thinking, and pissing off the government and other symbols of authority, including parents. The hippie philosophy embraced peace, love, and happiness. Most hippies got high, expressed love openly and freely, opposed government policies, protested the war in Vietnam, and lived in the moment.

They adopted the phrase, "turn on, tune in, drop out," popularized by Timothy Leary, as a slogan encouraging people to embrace cultural change. The term "flower children" became synonymous with the first generation of hippies from the San Francisco Bay Area. Flower children were amongst the first wave of hippies who would go around passing out flowers to people, spreading love and kindness. Besides passing out flowers, they also adorned themselves with garlands of flowers in their hair.

As the budding young hippies experienced a new lifestyle and made up new rules for themselves, the concept of free love emerged, opening up a new awareness and attitude about sex and love. The free love philosophy created a trend of open sex—or at least open affection—with one, or more than one, partner at a time. Hippies embraced the idea of a universal love where everyone was deserving of love equally. The meaning of love seemed to expand and love was expressed in various ways, not always in a sexual way either. The boundaries of personal space opened up, and hippies hugged and kissed one another, held hands, and formed group hugs. Along with that came the act of staring deeply into another's eyes with a stargazed look.

Hallucinogenic drugs like LSD (acid), psilocybin mushrooms, peyote cactus buttons, hashish, and of course marijuana, all strongly influenced the early hippie culture. Folk music and rock and roll played important roles as well, just as much as the hippie culture influenced many artists and what they chose to sing about. Influential song lyrics sent messages of peace and love, and preached philosophies such as defending beliefs and changing the world into a place where everyone lived as one.

Around the mid to late '60s the first wave of hippies started having babies. The new counterculture now held responsibility for raising children, and they did so in a somewhat experimental way. As young parents, the early hippies were the ones to lay the foundation on how to raise children alternatively. As the young hippie parents journeyed through life discovering and experiencing their new values, ideologies, and lifestyle, their children more or less tagged along for the ride.

My Story

❧✿❧

My personal life story begins in the "Summer of Love," which is the common term used to describe the summer of 1967. The hippie movement was in full swing when my parents met and conceived me. From birth all the way through high school, I lived the classic "hippie kid" life.

I made my entrance into this world on February 20, 1968.The way I look at the concept of being born is that we come from one unknown in order to venture into another unknown. I was born in a hospital in San Mateo, California. It was still common in the sixties for hippies to give birth in a hospital. Starting in the '70s, most of the hippies embraced home births assisted by a mid-wife. Even so, my mom chose to have a "natural" childbirth. Instead of using the drugs commonly administered to women in labor, my mom ate a gram of hashish.

My parents named me Anastasia Galadriel Machacek. I am the offspring of a stereotypical seventeen-year-old flower-child mom who was born and raised in the Bay area. My dad was more of the beatnik type, from the beat generation. The beatniks were the pre-hippie movement non- conformists who hung out in coffee shops listening to jazz music, reciting poetry and held philosophical conversations. My dad was a professional photographer at the time. According to my mom, they conceived me in a dark room.

Daddy Bob 1969

Hippie Heritage

❦

Haight-Ashbury, free concerts in Golden Gate Park, UC Berkley, LSD, free love, The Grateful Dead, Janis Joplin, The Beatles, and Bob Dylan; paisley patterned clothes, flowing skirts, bare feet, long hair (on both men and women), beads and tie-dyes; late-night philosophical coffeehouse discussions, war protests, pot smoking, and chess matches: these all stood as signs of the times from the era in which I was born.

When I was born, my parents lived in the San Francisco Bay Area in a place called "Hippie Hollow," where a bunch of hippies had settled in little cottages. My February birthdate made me a Pisces, right on the cusp of Aquarius. Hippies loved discussing astrology in those days. In fact, "What's your sign?" was an iconic conversation starter. Hippies also enjoyed discussing other mind-stimulating topics of philosophy, spirituality, metaphysics, and yoga. They pondered questions about God, our existence, and the meaning of life over cups of coffee and marijuana cigarettes.

My status as a Pisces might not be a big deal today, but for someone raised around a bunch of hippies who based their reality and outlook on life on the influences of the stars, it mattered quite a bit. Everyone in those days seemed to know an astrologer. Astrologers researched all the data surrounding the time and place of a person's birth and would chart out the planets and the signs they passed through at that exact time. They would then come up with an interpretation of what that meant and how those signs might influence an individual's personality.

Each astrological sign has its own properties and characteristics. People born under Pisces, the sign of the fish, are said to be highly sensitive, intuitive, and emotional. Astrology is still popular in today's society.

As I said, my parents named me Anastasia, which harkens back to the famous Russian princess and daughter of Czar Nicholas II. My middle name, Galadriel, came from an elf queen in J. R. R. Tolkien's *The Lord of the Rings*. It was challenging for me to carry around such an unusual name that no one could ever pronounce! So, for most of my childhood everyone just called me Ana. Even then I was faced with always having to correct people. Most everyone wanted to pronounce my name as "Anne- ah" I would then correct them and say, " Ah- nah". The A's in my name have a soft sound like in "father", not the nasal sounding A in "dad".

Once I got to high school some of my friends started to call me Anastasia, after they discovered what my full name actually was. Everyone said it was "such a cool name". Hey, at least I wasn't named Waterfall, Star shine, or Butterfly. A lot of hippies in those days tended to name their kids unusual names, not realizing the difficulty it could cause getting them accepted into mainstream society, though maybe that was the idea. For those attending public school, blending in could be hard enough without having a strange name that could be easily mocked. How embarrassing for a child to have to endure the ridicule of a name like Singing River, Morning Blossom, or Sunflower. Most hippies took their inspiration for names from other cultures, like The Native Americans, as well as African and East Indian traditions where names hold symbolic meaning and represent things from nature, a concept, or a particular god or goddess.

Stereotypes, Hippie Icons, and Music

❧❀❧

S omewhere along the line, the word "hippie" became associated with being dirty and smoking pot. Perhaps this stereotyping started early on in the '60s when this new generation of visionaries, rebels, idealists, and revolutionists started to grow out their hair, camped out at music festivals, didn't bathe for days at a time, and smoked pot openly. Because of their radical differences, conservatives and mainstream society coined the phrase "dirty long-haired hippie" to describe the no longer clean-cut youths. Hippies gathered together, held peace rallies, and formed communes. They dressed in colorful attire, rebelling in fashion and creating frenzy in a perfect *Leave it to Beaver* society. Paisley, patchouli oil, pot smoking, long hair, bare feet and free love all became synonymous with the hippie lifestyle.

In reality, most hippies were highly educated and clean. Many of the original hippie icons were actually a well-respected intellectual group of individuals. A few of the leading pioneers of the hippie movement which I am familiar with included Timothy Leary, who was a Harvard professor

11

and one of the leading advocates for experimenting with LSD. A man named Ram Dass had a significant influence on the hippie culture through bringing awareness of spirituality, metaphysics, meditation and yoga with his book: *Be Here Now*. Famous author Ken Kesey was an advocate for the use of psychedelic drugs. Evidently, he took part in government drug research experiments with psychoactive drugs including LSD. Kesey and a group of his friends, the merry pranksters became well known for being associated with experimenting and providing LSD in mass quantities to large groups of people, which had a big impact on the early hippie culture. A San Francisco State University professor, Stephen Gaskin was most famous for his Monday night talks on various thought-provoking subjects like politics, sex, and mind expansive drugs like LSD. In the early '70s he started one of the first hippie communes called The Farm, in Tennessee.

Another icon that influenced the early hippies was Wavy Gravy. Wavy Gravy was (and still is) the most famous hippie clown of all times. A radical, entertaining, and colorful character that wore tie-dye shirts and clown pants when he spoke to crowds of people at festivals and Grateful dead shows. Wavy Gravy started a Children's camp program called, Camp Winnarainbow, where hippie kids could learn how to juggle, do various circus acts, play, sing and dance. I am sure there are many others who also had an influence over the early hippie culture as well. These are just a few of the names that stand out in my mind in particular.

Credit—or blame—for the radical behavior of the hippies also lay with rock and roll and the messages it generated. One of the biggest legends of such influential music included the

Grateful Dead. The Grateful Dead developed such a loyal following of devoted fans that their concerts became more of an experience rather than just a rock concert. Hippies would camp out and party together for days at a time during a series of Dead shows. For many, it was customary to follow the Dead around on tour, traveling from city to city wherever the band would go. Those groupies became known as "Dead heads".

The Beatles also influenced the hippies with their style of feel good music, as well as, Bob Dylan, Jim Morrison, Jimi Hendrix and Janis Joplin, just to name a few. Drugs played a big role with influencing what singers and songwriters wrote and performed. Psychedelic drugs, heroin, cocaine, alcohol, and many other substances infiltrated into the music scene, opening up the opportunity for musicians to experiment with electrical technology like never before. Perhaps due to the effects of drugs, many musicians were inspired to push the limits and explore with sounds and create unique tones, straying away from the classic standards of music.

From a very early age I can recall that my parents always had music playing from records, or a reel-to-reel tape player. My favorites were The Beatles and The Rolling Stones. I also loved Joni Mitchell and Carly Simon. Both Cat Stevens and Bob Dylan inspired me to want to sing along with their records. Music made a big impression and influenced me from as far back as I can remember.

Music seemed to play an important role within the early hippie culture. Music brought people together. Music inspired and motivated people to explore and express their feelings and emotions freely. Perhaps listening to music while taking drugs somehow heightened the experience for many people as well.

Did you know?

1. Not all people who have long hair are hippies.
2. Not all hippies have long hair.
3. Some hippies do wear business suits and ties.
4. Not all hippies smoke pot.
5. Not all pot smokers are hippies.
6. Some hippie women do shave their legs and armpits.
7. Many hippies actually do use deodorant.
8. Not all people with dreadlocks are hippies.
9. Not all hippie men have beards.
10. Not all hippies are vegetarians.
11. Not all vegetarians are hippies.
12. Not all hippies collect welfare and food stamps.
13. Not all people who get welfare and food stamps are hippies.
14. A lot of hippies do pay taxes.
15. Most hippies do vote.
16. Not all hippies act "flakey" or "spaced out."
17. More than likely, most hippies do bathe regularly.
18. Not all hippies wear patchouli (some actually hate the smell).
19. Many hippies have attended and graduated college with honors and degrees.
20. Many movie stars, musicians and celebrities consider themselves hippies.

(Anastasia, 2008)

Psychedelic Experience

Most kids will take trips to Disneyland, or to the zoo. Hippie kids had a different experience behind the meaning of the word "trip." The hippies referred to an experience they had while taking LSD (acid) as "tripping." Users take a trip, but in their minds, through hallucinations. The experience can last several hours, or even an entire day or night. It was pretty common in those days when living amongst the hippies to partake in drugs, smoke pot, and trip openly in front of everyone, even children.

Two-and-a-half-year-old children really should not be exposed to such intensive, mind-altering substances as LSD. I, however, in my less-than-ideal situation, survived ingesting seven hits of pure microdot LSD. Being a typical, curious two-and-a-half-year-old who got into everything, I discovered the "carefully hidden" acid wrapped in tin foil in my mom's purse. I managed to ingest all seven doses before my parents realized what had happened. I must have told my mom I had eaten some candy, because once she figured out what I had done, she told me that I had eaten "magic candy." According to my mom, the LSD I took was of the purest concentrate produced by the legendary Owsley. A man name Owsley Stanley was one of the first to produce mass quantities of LSD out of Berkley during the '60s. As far as I know, LSD became an illegal substance by the fall of 1966.

It was 1970 when I had my first psychedelic experience. I was a typical two-and-a-half-year-old learning to converse and discovering what life was all about. After ingesting the acid I had discovered in my mom's purse I started to trip. My brain tried to process so many deep and intellectually-advanced thoughts for my years that I started to ponder concepts and ask questions that my parents couldn't answer, like, "Where do we come from?" and "How did we all get here?" When my parents simply answered with "God", I then began to ponder the concept and meaning of who and what was god? Those thoughts played over and over in my brain like a tape. Normal children my age most likely never considered such intense thoughts. I finally concluded that since I came from my mom, I must be her, only a different version, which led me to believe that everyone must be connected in some way.

I was living in Redwood City California with my mom and dad at the time. That acid trip remains my first, and most vivid, childhood memory. Because I was unable to comprehend the concept of time at that age, I have no real idea how long the experience lasted. Only the feelings, along with fragmented details, left an impression on me. The experience itself can only be explained in the simplest terms from my memory because I was so very young at the time.

My clearest memory of that day is of my dad holding me and carrying me around the house. As he carried me through the living room, I remember hearing music playing from the stereo. "Puff the Magic Dragon," sung by Peter, Paul, and Mary, rang out from the turntable. I distinctly remember contemplating the words to that song. When I heard the words "sealing wax…" I interpreted it as "ceiling wax." I recall staring at the ceiling and actually "seeing" wax drip in strands from the ceiling, just like wax dripping from a candlestick. Apparently that was the hallucination that my brain had conjured so vividly that I believed the ceiling was melting. Beyond that, I have no recollection of what went on that day.

"Me, Christmas 1970"

Current Thoughts on the Drug Issue...

ind-altering drugs may serve a purpose for someone, somewhere. I strongly believe that any kind of drug is not good inside of a child's body. Looking back on my early childhood acid experience now seems so unreal to me. As an adult, I think to myself, "No way! That couldn't possibly happen to a child!" Especially now as a parent, I cannot imagine a child at any age going through such an intense experience. I was definitely subjected to thoughts, ideas, feelings, and concepts far beyond my years.

I believe that my parents did the best they could to handle the situation. Because of the peaceful environment and the positive energy that surrounded me, I felt safe and calm under the circumstances. After all, as hippies my parents always acted mellow, happy, and laid-back.

Most hippie parents were pretty loose with their drug activities in those days. With pot as the most common drug of choice, many hippie kids grew up high on second-hand smoke, or else smoked joints themselves. I remember eating the "roaches" (the butts of the marijuana cigarettes) right out of the ashtray! I didn't do this very often because they tasted pretty bad and were difficult to swallow.

Accidental, or intentional, dosing of acid was probably not too common amongst hippie kids. As far as I ever knew, I wasn't aware of any other kids around me being dosed. I have heard from friends that their hippie moms took acid or smoked pot while breastfeeding. By doing this, they exposed their young ones to the effects of the mind-altering experience just the same.

I don't recall seeing drugs like heroin or cocaine during my childhood. Many hippie kids however, experienced the detrimental effects of their parents' addictions. Alcohol use and abuse made its way into the hippie culture as well. My dad struggled with alcoholism, which my mom opposed of. My mom always avoided alcohol herself, and seemed pretty judgmental toward people who drank. "Alcohol creates bad vibes and negative energy," she would say. She also claimed that "marijuana is not a drug, it is a botanical." In those days I think she believed that since it was not man-made in a pharmaceutical laboratory, it shouldn't be considered a drug.

Addressing a Touchy Issue...

The subject of inappropriate sexual misconduct involving adults and children should not be overlooked. Child molesters seem to infiltrate any and all levels of our society, regardless of economic, or social status, and the children of the hippie culture were not immune. Yes, hippie kids were just as prone to being molested by an adult as any other kid. Just to be clear, a pedophile will operate regardless of where they try to fit themselves into society. That is, unfortunately, a fact that cannot be avoided.

I chose to address this issue, not only to open up some awareness on the topic, but also to make it clear that there were many situations in my childhood where adults and children where running around naked together, as a natural way of life. Swimming in the rivers, taking saunas, or soaking in hot springs, adults and children were often naked together. It was an accepted part of the culture and considered normal. From most of my experiences, almost everyone was respectful and acted appropriately. The notion of free love and being openly affectionate with one another didn't usually cross the lines involving children.

In my case, I did unfortunately experience the lines being crossed on a few different occasions throughout my childhood. The first incident happened at the very young age of three, involving an adult male whose identity is still unknown to me. What I do recall from the incident is that I was sitting on a man's lap in the back of a van. It was evening and the van was parked. There were other people present who were getting in and out of the van. I couldn't really see anyone very well or the man whose lap I was on because it was dark. The man put his hand inside of my underwear and began touching my yoni (vagina) with his fingers. No one around was aware of what was going on, and I have no recollection of how long the incident went on for. As far as I know, this was a onetime occurrence. I never told anyone.

Later on during my childhood when I was about eight years old, I was sleeping over at a friend's house. Her parents had an old homeless man staying in their living room. In the middle of the night my friend went in to wake him up so that he would come in and "play" with us. I remember lying in her bed next to her as this old grandpa-aged guy got on top of her. I was really nervous and scared, not really sure what was going to happen next. After a few minutes had passed he then proceeded to lie on top of me! I just lay there very still, feeling his heavy body on top of me. I do recall that my nightgown was pulled up but I kept my underwear on and the man was also clothed. Even though there was clothing protecting me from his body parts, it felt disgusting having him on top of me. I believe he was trying to hump us, which made me feel really gross and disgusted by the whole incident. In my mind I knew that what he had done was wrong, yet I felt very embarrassed and ashamed to tell anyone about it afterward.

Not to minimize what I endured, but I know from stories told to me by others that scenarios involving pedophiles can vary. Regardless of the details, any and all inappropriate sexual misconduct or intention involving an adult crossing that line with children is unacceptable and wrong. I have heard several stories from others who also grew up within the hippie culture about their traumatic sexual abuse as children. They had to survive through repeated inappropriate sexual molestation with actual penetration by someone their parents knew. More than likely their experiences were horrific and life altering, to say the least.

I know that for me personally, I have had to suppress the feelings of guilt and shame. I have had the burden of harboring the secret that I was sexually violated at such a young age. The way I chose to process what happened to me almost excuses the perpetrators. I minimized the incidents so they didn't seem so bad. I would tell myself that it really wasn't so traumatic because at least no one actually put their penis inside of me. I now realize that is where I have been wrong. Being touched inappropriately was a violation to me and caused me to experience feelings and process concepts children should never endure.

Occasionally hippie parents would neglectfully and carelessly leave their children to fend for themselves while they went off to get high or "get it on," putting their kids in a vulnerable situation. Under these circumstances, hippie kids also explored their own sexuality with each other. Often the older children would take advantage of younger ones. I was only four years old when I had my first sex play experience with another boy my age. I had seen my parents making love before, so I was aware of the process, at least from what my young mind was able to interpret.

Another Trip

❧

S hortly after I turned three years old my mom and dad split up. My mom started seeing a new boyfriend whom we went to live with. He lived in a small one-bedroom house near the beach, just north of San Francisco. I do remember that my mom's new boyfriend had a motor-cycle with a sidecar attached to it. On the weekends he would take us for rides along the coast. At one point the two of them took off on a cross-country road trip while I stayed with my dad for a month.

One morning when I was three and a half, my mom cooked breakfast in the tiny kitchen of our new house. I helped her by getting things out of the refrigerator. My mom asked me to get some eggs for her to cook. I remember opening the fridge door and looking inside. There weren't that many items in the fridge, it was rather bare. I saw the eggs, but I also noticed sitting right there in front of me on the wire shelf a small strip of red win-dowpane LSD. Windowpane LSD is a type of acid, which came in the form of small gelatin squares. This particular type was colored red. I didn't hesitate to pop the "candy" into my mouth.

I quickly ate the three squares of windowpane acid and handed my mom the eggs. She had no idea what I had done. I don't even know that I knew what I had done, for that matter. I didn't start tripping until after breakfast when we went out to the store. We had stopped at a nearby produce stand to pick up some fruit and vegetables when I started to laugh hysterically. I don't have a very detailed memory of what exactly occurred.

After we got back into our car, I began to have an intense trip with hallucinations. I kept seeing my mom's foot go through the floorboards of the car as she pushed the pedals to drive, and I kept laughing. Everything looked like a cartoon, and I felt like my entire body was melting into the seat of the car. I realized at that point what was happening to me, and I told my mom that I had eaten "magic candy." Beyond that, I have no recollection of what my mom said, how she reacted, or how the rest of my trip went.

Commune Living

During the time of my parents' separation, it was decided that I was to live with my mom. More than likely their decision to separate came about because they just simply grew apart. Problems also started to arise once they began to explore the whole experience of free love and open marriage. Both people in an open marriage have the freedom to explore intimate relationships outside of the marriage with other partners. My mom didn't want to share my dad with anyone else. Besides, she had a different path in life to pursue. A much stronger force guided her to experience the New Age of spirituality.

My mom took me with her on her journey to seek an alternative lifestyle through the New Age of awareness. I had my first hippie commune experience at Wheeler's Ranch. It sat on a 320-acre piece of property located in Sonoma County near Occidental, California, where several hippie families and individuals had created an alternative living community. Hippie communes were springing up all over the country. At Wheeler's Ranch, people lived in tree houses, cabins, tents, and shacks. People constructed various structures from the simplest form like a lean-to with tarps draped over wooden structures with dirt flooring to elaborate log cabins with windows and plywood floors. The only source of running water was from a garden hose, which was centrally located for folks to fill water jugs to carry back to their homes. As far as I know, the ranch didn't have electricity. Clothing was optional, and many chose to exercise their right to wear little or no clothing at all. Many parents gave their kids the freedom to run around naked, which they considered the natural and accepted norm.

Commune living entailed a very simplistic, back-to-the-land lifestyle. Communes strived to create a community where people could live in harmony with like-minded individuals, ideally living self-sufficiently, independent of the government and society at large. Commune members contributed what they could: money, skills, and labor. Hippies from all different backgrounds joined communes. Many came from families with lots of money, bringing trust funds with them. Others had nothing. In spite of the best intentions, however, it was pretty typical for members to collect welfare and food stamps, which is kind of a contradiction, since the hippies all tried to rebel against the government and have nothing to do with the "system".

Wheeler's Ranch was named after a guy named Bill Wheeler, who dedicated his property to God. I believe this meant that no one person had the right to actually own the earth and that it was god's land. Word spread quickly that Wheeler's Ranch was open to anyone who was inspired to live off the land and held the same vision of living as equals, sharing common beliefs of respecting one another and the earth. As well as, living in a way that was disconnected from the government and mainstream society. Lots of hippies flocked from the San Francisco Bay Area, other parts of California and most likely other parts of the country as well, to live on this remote, difficult-to-access commune.

In order to reach the commune, we had to hike a long way (at least two or three miles) through a steep canyon, or else catch a ride on the commune's big flatbed truck. Motorized vehicles were not allowed onto the property. Even the community truck could only make scheduled town runs because the access road went through the neighboring property of an uptight sheep rancher who absolutely did not like all those hippies living next to him, let alone passing through his property. In fact, many people tried to sneak through his property during the night, only to get picked up by the cops.

I recall the times when we would all pile onto the back of the flatbed truck to venture into town for a "town run." People went for various reasons: to stock up on food and supplies, to do laundry, to make phone calls to family and check their post office boxes, to cash welfare checks or collect food stamps. I remember pulling into the parking lot of a big grocery store and jumping off the back of the truck as part of the mob of hippies.

Some town trips turned into bigger adventures to San Francisco. My mom earned money as a belly dancer. Sometimes we would go to Ghirardelli Square and my mom would have some musician friends play music while she danced. I worked as the little panhandler. "Spare change for my mom, the Belly dancer!" I would call. Standing on the sidewalk and filling my pockets with change from passing strangers as my mom entertained the crowds with her dancing could hardly be considered normal preschool behavior. But I was a hippie kid, just a bit out of the norm to begin with.

Psychedelic Road Trip

I was four years old during the very first Rainbow Gathering held on National Forest Service land in Colorado in 1972. I will never forget the road trip from California to Colorado. A van full of hippies from Wheeler's Ranch took the adventure of a lifetime into the Rocky Mountains of Colorado with sleeping bags, backpacks, pillows, camping gear, one canteen filled with orange juice laced with LSD, and one four-year-old child. (That was me!)

The back of the van did not have any seats. Everyone just piled in and sat on all of the gear wherever they could. As the van chugged down the road, pot smoke billowed out from the windows (similar to an image from a Cheech and Chong movie). At some point someone pulled out the canteen of juice laced with LSD and started passing it around for everyone to drink. I am not sure where in the van my mom sat at the time. She may have been driving or sitting up front. I'm not even sure whether or not she participated in the tripping. As far as I know, she had no idea that anyone had passed the canteen to me. After taking a drink of the juice, I started to feel that strange, distinctive tripping feeling come on. I had been dosed, and started to trip along with everyone else in the van. As I look back on that now, I find myself asking the question: wasn't anyone paying attention? I was the only child amongst a group of young adult hippies who, according to my calculations now, were anywhere from sixteen years old to mid-twenties—practically still children themselves.

I most vividly recall the feeling of not recognizing my body as solid matter. My body felt like cotton candy, all fluffy and invisible. I stared down at the palms of my hands and saw the lines swirl together. This was way more intense for me than the first time I had tripped at two years old. To make the experience even more traumatic and life altering, we got into a car accident. At that point I had moved up front to ride on someone's lap. Of course in those days, seat belt laws didn't exist. Who knows if the van even had seat belts? I know that I didn't use one. I don't know all of the details of the accident exactly, but I do remember hearing the screech of the tires, feeling the van swerve, and watching us cross over the entire road to the oncoming lanes of traffic.

The van came to a sudden, jolting stop with the front driver's-side wheel hanging over the edge of a cliff. Seconds before the van miraculously came to its abrupt stop, the entire group of tripping passengers, all higher than kites, simultaneously yelled, "STOP!" In some unexplainable way, that may be what kept the van full of hippies from going over the cliff. The cliff dropped straight down, hundreds of feet into a ravine, with the Colorado River below.

By some miracle, no one got hurt. I truly believe guardian angels protected us. After the van came to its sudden stop, everyone piled out onto the side of the road. Gathering all of their strength, they worked together to lift the front end of the van back up onto the road. What a sight it must have been to the average family passing by the scene of that accident as they drove their family station wagon through the Rocky Mountains on summer vacation. Slowing down to pass the accident scene, the lady in the car would probably turn to her husband to say, "Look Carl, what are those hippies doing with that van?" Her husband would respond, "Oh Marge, that's probably just some hippie car ritual. They all must be high on something." And indeed we were.

My memories of the Rainbow Gathering itself are vague. I do remember pulling into a big parking lot out in the middle of the wilderness. Feeling relieved to finally get out of the van; I had no idea what was in store for me next. In order to reach the location of the gathering, we had to hike straight up an incredibly steep mountain. My concept of distance could not comprehend the hike as being more or less than one mile. To a four-year-old, the hike seemed endless and painfully treacherous. Imagine a four-year-old who had just spent several hours tripping on acid and almost going over a cliff in a van! After that traumatic experience, I felt vulnerable and exhausted, to say the least.

As we began the journey trudging up the steep mountain through the woods, I quickly became weak and started to complain. Groups of hippies loaded down with backpacks, camping gear and supplies strode up the mountain with eagerness and excitement to reach their destination. I threw the biggest temper tantrum by crying hysterically. Refusing to continue the hike I sat down beside the path and started to cry. My mom couldn't carry me, since she was loaded down with all of our camping gear. She kept on hiking and left me by the side of the trail, crying. Having my mom leave me sitting there, alone crying made me furious. I realized that I had no choice but to keep on walking. Struggling every step of the way, with aching feet and wobbly legs I eventually made it to the top of the mountain. Somehow, I found the strength to endure the intense pain of the hike. I did manage to get some sympathy from a concerned, caring hippie guy who gave me a piggyback ride part of the way up the steep mountain trail.

I have no detailed memories of the Rainbow Gathering itself. Those memories are all fragmented or lost. Most likely I was recovering from the traumatic road trip that brought us there. I can vaguely remember crowds of people sitting around campfires, playing music and chanting, wandering around meadows, exploring the wilderness, and playing with other kids. Once the gathering ended and it was time to go home, I threw another tantrum. I vividly recall not wanting to ride back in the van. I refused to go through the same experience again! My mom arranged for me to ride back to California with my friend Grasshopper and her parents, in their station wagon. My mom chose to ride back home in the same van we rode in to get there.

The road trip home was a much better experience for me. Having other kids in the car made me feel at ease. More importantly, no one handed me a canteen full of juice laced with LSD. I don't remember any of the details of the return trip to California, but I did manage to make it safely back home to my mom at Wheeler's Ranch.

Big Sur Cave Dwelling

❧

We moved away from Wheeler's Ranch before the government came in and condemned all of the buildings, bulldozing everyone's homes. Apparently the structures were not built to code. Luckily, we got out of there before the brutal destruction. Somehow we ended up living in a cave in Big Sur. That's right, a cave.

Big Sur is located on the central coast of California. My mom and her new boyfriend at the time, who was from Germany, claimed a secluded little area on a rocky beach. There was a house on the cliffs above where some friend's of ours lived. Our temporary home was constructed on a wooden platform in front of a little cave, nestled amongst giant boulders. The structure itself was covered with clear plastic tarps. In a sense, it was kind of like camping. The entire structure enclosed the cave entrance, making the cave an adjoining room for storage. Our "house" was pretty difficult to access. We had to climb down a steep cliff to a rocky beach and climb on big boulders to get home. When it rained, we stayed huddled up inside, as the rains could be heavy and the wind strong. The rain pounded so loudly that it seemed like the ocean itself was crashing against our plastic shelter that protected us from the elements. Those heavy, violent, thundering waves during a storm scared me.

We moved to Big Sur so that my mom could further her education in holistic healing by studying at The Esalen Institute for Healing. She studied massage therapy, and other healing arts as well. I remember going to Esalen with her and soaking in the hot springs that overlooked the Pacific Ocean from the cliffs. After my mom completed her courses of study at Esalen, she decided that we should move to Hawaii. My mom painted bathrooms in an apartment building in order to save enough money for our plane tickets. I was almost five years old when we left on our adventure to the Hawaiian Islands.

Hawaii

❀

As my childhood travels took us to live in Hawaii, I had no idea what adventures that would bring. To a five-year-old hippie kid, living in the jungles on the island of Maui was just a normal way to live. In those days, the homeless hippies in Hawaii lived on the beach or found a place to set up a tent out in the jungle. We did just that. For a few months, we camped out in the jungle on some friend's property. Our makeshift lean-to nestled amongst the trees near a river was where we called home. In order to access the main house or to reach the road to go into to town, we had to wade across a river.

One memory, which stands out for me during the time we lived on that part of the island, occurred during a tropical storm. The ceaseless downpour of heavy rain went on for days, causing everything to get drenched, including our improvised "home" of sheet plastic and tarps strung between the trees (kind of like our home in the cave back in California). The water level in the river rose, and the current became so strong we couldn't cross to the other side to seek shelter within our friend's home. I remember trying to wade through the rushing water, but it was far too dangerous. With the currents so strong, the river nearly swept us under. We had no choice but to turn back and wait it out until the rains stopped and the river levels went down. For several days we huddled together in our plastic-draped shelter in the jungle trying to stay dry. Our food supply consisted of trail mix, dried fruit, sprouts, and fresh tropical fruits like bananas, avocados, and papayas. The torrential rains finally ceased after what seemed to be forever, and we were able to dry ourselves out. Shortly after that experience, we moved to a different part of the island.

My mom met an old, local Hawaiian man who owned some property in Wailua Valley, just off the Hana Highway in a very remote part of the island out in the jungle. The structure we lived in had once functioned as a poi-manufacturing factory. The owners had abandoned it years before we moved in. With their permission, we made the place our home. We had to hitchhike to go into town for supplies. Tourists or locals would always stop and give us a ride.

The turn to get to the access road to reach our "house" operated as a tourist lookout spot where visitors would pull over to view the beautiful, lush jungle and take photographs. Sightseers couldn't see the abandoned factory from the road. We had to walk a bit of a distance (maybe a half mile) in order to reach our home. I recall being surrounded by groves of guava and papaya trees as we walked throughout the property. We were able to gather and eat fresh fruit all of the time. A short walk from where we lived sat a magical, hidden, freshwater pool with a cascading waterfall. A rose apple tree grew by the river, with fruit similar to an apple with a distinct flavor like the fragrance of a rose. Plumeria and gardenia flowers filled the air with their unforgettably powerful aromas.

During the time we lived in Wailua Valley, the weather stayed consistently warm and sunny. We spent our days gathering fruit as we walked through the lush jungle to the peaceful swimming hole. I would jump off the rocks into the pool and swim around like a little fish. It was our private place in paradise. Then the rainy season came, and the rains wouldn't let up for days. In spite of the wet and rainy weather, I still remember unusual warmth. The structure we lived in had a tin roof, a common feature in Hawaii. The sound of the rain beating down echoed so loudly as it hit the roof that it drowned out all other sounds. At times, the rain would abruptly stop and the sun would burst out, creating a calm, comforting feeling, as if the violence of all the rain had never existed.

During one particular storm, my mom and I set out for a typical walk through the jungle to visit with a neighbor (some hippie guy who lived in a shack with his goat on the other side of the river). Our usual walk that day turned into an adventure of a lifetime. We walked along the familiar path leading to the swimming hole. As we approached the river, we saw that the rains had caused the water level to rise significantly. The sweet, gentle stream and soft, flowing waterfall had become intensely fierce and loud. The beautiful, clear pool had turned turbulent and muddy. The river rushed with rage. Our peaceful, quaint, serene swimming hole tried to swallow us up. We needed to cross at the top of the waterfall, where we always had. In order to reach the other side, my mom put me up on her shoulders and began to cross the river. In a split second, the strong current swept us over the waterfall!

Everything happened so quickly; I didn't even have time to feel scared. Though my eyes were open, everything passed in a blur. The waterfall had a gradual descent, like a slide, because it had been a lava tube. The only sudden drop came at the very bottom, which poured into the pool. Once the river dumped us into the pool, I could see the blurry image of my mom under the water in front of me. She reached out for me, and we both came up to the surface. Once again, I believe that I had my guardian angel watching over me. I was a little shaky after that, but I survived unharmed and surprisingly not too freaked-out by the whole incident. We managed to make our way over to the neighbor's shack and spent the night there.

One thing I do recall about the locals is that Hawaiians were not very fond of people running around naked. For a couple of months we rented a room in a house in the town of Wailuku. I can remember playing out in the yard, running around naked and the Hawaiian neighbors would yell out over the fence: "shame, shame, shame, where's your panties?" After hearing them say that I would run into the house feeling embarrassed. From that point on, I became aware of my modesty.

On several occasions my mom took me to participate in the Hare Krishna temple activities. I enjoyed that, since they served good food and sang songs and played music. A lot of hippies joined the Hare Krishna movement, which was a religious organization based on Hindu scriptures, honoring the Hindu god Krishna. We participated in the meetings by singing and listening to the readings, but never officially joined the organization. My mom was into exploring all aspects of spirituality and interested in what the New Age had to offer.

Tripping on Acid at the Beach

～❀～

During that year of living in Hawaii, I got dosed once again with LSD. Yes, that's right, again. We went with a group of people, including a bunch of other kids, to Makenna Beach, where big waves roll onto an endless beach. A rocky cliff separated the beach into two parts. One side of the beach was called "big beach" and the other side was called "little beach". Little beach was where all the hippies could go and swim naked. That day we stayed on big beach.

I remember riding out to the beach in a VW bus. Once everyone got out of the vehicle, some guy passed out dried fruit leather laced with LSD. Each person, including all of the kids, ate a portion of those "treats." As soon as I started to trip, I knew what was happening. I knew that this feeling was not my normal state of being. I recognized the intensely strange sensations taking over my body. From my past experiences, I was somewhat familiar and able to figure out that my perception of reality was being altered. At that point I knew that this feeling would last for the rest of the day. I remember thinking to myself that I had no control over what was happening and

I had to just give in to the sensations and know that it would eventually be over.

I spent the entire time walking up and down the beach. At one point I began turning around in circles as I walked. I would turn one way and feel like I was getting bigger, like a reel of film. Then I would turn the opposite direction and feel as if I were "unwinding" and getting smaller. I also stood and stared out into the ocean, watching the waves as they came in and went back out. The flies that flew around me left tracers in the air, and I tripped out on that for a very long time.

I really don't know what the other kids did or what they experienced. How could anyone think it was a good idea to dose the kids anyway? And, to top it off, with all of the adults tripping too, who watched out for the kids? I know my mom stayed close to me and watched out to be sure I stayed safe, at least once she realized I had been dosed.

Oregon

❦

After living in Hawaii for about a year, we moved to Oregon. I think my mom fell in love with some hippie tourist who lived on a hippie commune somewhere in Oregon. Just west of Eugene, near a town called Veneta, there was a little hippie commune called Mirkwood. We ended up living there on and off for a couple of years. The name Mirkwood was inspired from the book, *The Hobbit by J.R.R. Tolkein.*

Mirkwood included several little cabins nestled throughout the woods, along with some tepees. As on most hippie communes, vehicles could not access the property beyond the parking lot. Some people actually lived in buses or vans parked out in the parking area. Hippies often converted old school busses into a type of mobile home. I had a few friends throughout my childhood who lived with their families in converted busses. Some busses had cool features, such as bunk beds, tie-dyed curtains, and wood burning stoves.

Mirkwood mostly consisted of young couples at the time. I was one of the only kids, other than a few babies born at home. Visitors came out to Mirkwood all the time, bringing their kids with them. There were always lots of other hippie kids around for me to play with. I also made friends with the kids who lived next door. Even though the neighbors weren't hippies, they were very hippie-friendly. In fact, they would let us come over to use their phone whenever anyone had to make an important call. Mirkwood didn't have a telephone.

The main house had electricity and running water with an outdoor shower for communal use. The cabins had no electricity. Some of the dwellings did have running water, but none had indoor bathrooms. Everyone contributed to two huge, communal, organic gardens. Mostly those who liked to garden helped by digging, planting, weeding, and harvesting. My mom was an avid gardener and spent a lot of time gardening. I enjoyed helping out in the garden alongside her.

Everyone contributed to the single communal outhouse as well. There was no formal structure, just a simple hole dug in the ground with boards over it for squatting. We had to pour a scoop of ashes from a bucket located next to the "shitter" into the hole after finishing our business. Since it didn't include any shelter, the surrounding trees and the branches above kind of created a little privacy. Sometimes there wasn't any toilet paper available and we had to improvise with leaves. The idea may sound a bit gross, but it was one of those things that hippies living out in the woods had to adapt to.

The first cabin we lived in was a bit of an adventure to access. It required a long walk up a little dirt path through the woods and into a meadow. It was quite a long distance from the parking lot and main house. The cabin consisted of one big room with a loft. We had to climb up a ladder to get to the loft, which was where my mom and her boyfriend slept. I had a little corner of the room downstairs with a mat on the floor, a pretty typical sleeping arrangement for me. Outside we would get our water from an old well. We used a little bucket tied to a rope to haul water to the surface. Sometimes the buckets got loose from the rope and we had to use a fishing pole to fish out the buckets.

Mirkwood Family, early '70s
Photo taken by Gary St. Martin

The Temple

❦

When I started to attend school, we moved into a cabin closer to the main house. It was an easier walk for me to get to the main road from there. I still had to walk down a gravel road for a ways, past cow pastures in order to catch the school bus. Residents referred to the house we moved into as the Temple. They used the Temple as the gathering place for meetings, potlucks, prayer circles, and ceremonial "sweats," with a communal sweat lodge right outside our front door.

Lots of hippies in those days integrated Native American traditions into their way of life, such as vision quests, prayer circles, chanting, tepee living, and ceremonial sweats. The idea behind the sweat lodge experience is to cleanse and purify the body and spirit by offering up prayers with chanting, singing, and drumming.

Tree branches are constructed to form the dome of a sweat lodge structure, which is then wrapped with tarps and wool blankets to keep the heat in. Rocks are heated in a fire pit outside of the sweat lodge, brought in with a shovel, and placed inside the structure. Everyone sits inside and sweats, as water is poured over the rocks to create steam. Huddled together inside this dark steamy place, everyone starts chanting, singing ceremonial peace songs, and "oming," which is a sound sung with various tones and intensities. "Ohhhhhhmmmmmmm". (When a group of hippies is "oming," it sounds like a bunch of cows mooing backwards).

Of course, no one wore a bathing suit into a sweat lodge. To a hippie kid, this was the normal way of life, and everyone accepted it as appropriate and acted accordingly.

Our house was constructed with rough-cut wood, log cabin-style. The layout consisted of one big, open, octagon-shaped room with a low ceiling, a dirt floor, lots of windows, and beautiful stained glass on the front door. We had a cast iron woodstove in the middle of our house that we used for heat. We also had an old-fashioned cast iron cooking stove with an oven in the kitchen area. My mom would bake really good bread and cakes in that old oven. The sink had running water, but it was only cold water from a hose. We had to boil water on the stove in order to wash the dishes. The house had no electricity at all. At night, we lit candles and lanterns to see.

I watched childbirth for the first time at Mirkwood. Hippies almost always had their babies at home with a mid-wife assisting. Whenever a lady went into labor, everyone would gather around to watch, like it was a party or something. Sometimes people would sing and play music, beat the drum, or chant. I just sat back and watched the whole amazing experience and the wonder of a new life entering the world.

One Big Family

❧

ippies viewed one another as brothers and sisters. In fact, they commonly addressed each other as "brother" or "sister" in the middle of a conversation, perhaps to manifest the ideal society where everyone lived as equals in one, big, happy family. Hippies gave a whole new meaning to the word family. As for actual family units, (i.e., mom, dad, and kids), many different possibilities existed (and still do). It was common for a man and woman to live together, have a couple of kids and then separate. When hippies did marry, their nontraditional weddings often happened out in a meadow or on a mountaintop somewhere. But not all hippie couples got married. Some preferred a little ceremony in front of friends and didn't choose to make it legal with all the paperwork. I often heard people using the terms "old man" and "ole' lady" to address their spouse instead of using the traditional "husband" and "wife" titles.

Women often would have several children to different fathers, causing families to split apart. Men too, would father children with more than one woman. Commitment and faithfulness didn't seem to rank very high on the list of priorities for the young hippies in those days. The hippies explored the endless possibilities of sexual freedom and expression, and what those ideas meant for them at the time. This led to carelessness and unintended pregnancies, causing some women to have babies without knowing the identity of the father, and for many men to father children without realizing it. As a result, many single mothers raised hippie kids on their own. Some kids never even knew their own fathers.

In some cases, one parent held more conservative views and didn't live the hippie lifestyle. In my case in particular, my dad was far more conservative-minded than my mom. Going to visit my dad in California was a rare event, so my visits with him were special to me. In order for me to even see him, my mom and I would hitchhike from Oregon to California about once a year. I would usually spend about a week with my dad, giving me a break from my unusual hippie environment. He would take me shopping at a mall for clothes; we would go to the movies, and out to eat at restaurants. During my teens we lost touch with my dad and I didn't reunite with him until I turned twenty-one years old.

After my mom and dad separated, my mom raised me on her own. Throughout my childhood it was just the two of us. We had such an extended network of friends wherever we went, and I often dubbed close friends of ours as being my "aunt" or "uncle". My mom did have various relationships with men for different lengths of time but never remarried after leaving my dad. I never had a stepfather or a strong father figure in my life.

I always looked forward to visiting relatives, like my grandma, my aunts, uncles, and cousins. For myself, and probably with other hippie kids, it was a bit of a culture shock to visit the homes of relatives who lived in normal houses. It was very different from the rustic settings of living in a hippie commune, or being homeless. I actually enjoyed visiting my relatives very much and was impressed with the luxuries and amenities that their modern fancy homes had. Having plush wall-to-wall carpet, electricity, and bathrooms with flushing toilets and beautiful color-coordinated matching towels and mats were impressive to me.

One of my favorite relatives to visit was my cousin Laurie. She lived in Huntington Beach, California with my Aunt Jeanette and Uncle Ed. Every time I visited I always wished that I could stay there and live with them. Maybe it had a lot to do with the fact they had a swimming pool and Jacuzzi in their backyard. My cousin Laurie had her own room, which she let me stay in whenever I visited. I always felt in awe of her and all the things she had: makeup, posters, a mirror, a dresser, lots of clothes, a lava lamp, a hair dryer, a curling iron, and, best of all, her very own waterbed!

I suppose the reason that my visits to see my cousin left such an impression on me is because of the fact that her life-style was the extreme opposite from my own. Perhaps the way my relatives lived, how their house looked, and the food they ate, somehow set a standard of normalcy for me. Besides, they were all so much fun, and exciting to be around.

First Grade

❀

"Mom, I want to go to a real school."

"Are you sure?" she would answer. "You really want to go to a structured institution, where they brainwash kids into believing all sorts of made-up lies? Where they stifle your creativity and form your personality to be a follower and not think for yourself?" Then she would add, "Besides, they feed the kids junk food that is so bad for you. White bread, meat, and white sugar shit."

"I don't care! I still want to go."

She intended to home school me herself, like most of the hippie kids I knew. That was part of being a hippie. A lot of hippies didn't send their kids off to public institutions to get brainwashed by the mainstream propaganda and forced to conform to the evil ways of society.

Somehow I convinced my mom to let me go to the local public school just down the road from Mirkwood. She usually let me do whatever I wanted anyway, so it didn't take much convincing on my part really. My mom gave in and said, "Okay, we'll give it a try, and see how it goes."

I started first grade just after Christmas break. So not only was I the new kid, but I had missed the first three months of first grade. Not to mention, I was the hippie kid of the school. None of the other kids lived out in the woods on a hippie commune. They all had TVs, indoor bathrooms, electricity, and hot lunches from the school cafeteria. Going to school every day felt like a real treat for me. It allowed me to escape into the normal world. The classroom had heat (not by a woodstove, either), I made some friends pretty easily, and I got to drink milk every day as my snack. The staff brought cute little cartons of white or chocolate milk to the classroom and passed them out to all of the kids.

I knew that my mom didn't want me to drink milk. She had pretty strict rules on the health-food issue. According to her, milk was the worst dairy product for you. Baby cows can easily digest cow's milk, but humans' digestive systems aren't designed to digest cow's milk as easily. My mom would always say that milk creates too much mucus. She didn't like the combination of bread and cheese, either. People used to ask, "How do you get your calcium if you don't drink milk?" My mom would answer, "Carrot juice, nuts and seeds, dark leafy greens, and a balanced, healthy diet." She gave the same answer whenever someone tried to give me a hard time about being a vegetarian. "So, no meat? What do you have for a hamburger, just the bun and some lettuce? What about getting enough protein?" As a kid, I shouldn't have had to justify and explain the beneficial health concepts of the vegetarian diet to ignorant grown-ups.

But even though I knew better, I drank the milk offered at school, enjoying every last drop of it—especially the chocolate! I wondered how any harm could come of it. I figured that my mom would never find out. Little did I know a bill would come home at the end of the school year? A dime for every carton of milk I drank? My mother had less of an issue with the money owed than with the fact that I had actually drunk cow's milk. I had tainted my picture-perfect, pure vegetarian diet.

Surprisingly, my mom didn't get all that upset with me over the whole issue. My mom rarely got mad at me. That's one of the benefits of being a hippie kid. Hippie parents didn't tend to discipline their kids too harshly. Usually I would just get a little lecture. "It's your body," my mom would say. She'd provide a few stern words of wisdom, combined with positive alternatives for choices to make. For behaviors like a temper tantrum, tears and such, she would say, "Calm down, watch your breath." I knew exactly what she meant: concentrate, calmly breathe, and be aware of my thoughts. That was my mom's firm and direct approach to positive discipline. Sometimes I would sarcastically say to my mom, "I am breathing. If I weren't, I would be dead!" Or, when it was cold outside and I could actually see my breath as the warm air from my lungs mixed with the cold air like clouds of smoke, I would say, "See, I am watching my breath."

Oh, the Humiliation!

❖

Surprisingly, I had a good experience in first grade, and I loved going to school. Except for lunchtime. The majority of the kids who attended Central Elementary School ate hot lunches from the school cafeteria. Just bringing my own "cold lunch" from home made me stand out from the rest of the kids. To top it off, my lunches weren't even normal. Instead of white bread and bologna sandwiches with whatever else kids considered acceptable at the time, my hippie-kid, health food lunches consisted of vegetarian sandwiches with alfalfa sprouts prepared on homemade, whole-grain brown bread, the slices cut thick and uneven with hearty crusts. The other kids would tease me and say, "Eewww! You have worms on your sandwich!" as they pointed and laughed at me. They had never eaten alfalfa sprouts before.

I realized then, the difference between me and other kids. I had been isolated up until then, protected from the harsh judgments of others. Most everyone I had known ate sprouts, or at least knew of them. "Are those leaves from a tree?" the kids would ask, in reference to the big leaf of lettuce on my sandwich. Hadn't they ever even eaten lettuce before? Apparently, the organically grown leafy lettuce from our garden was not the acceptable kind of lettuce.

If I didn't bring those horrid sprout sandwiches for lunch, I would have peanut butter sandwiches instead. Not the smooth, creamy, Skippy peanut butter with grape jelly on white Wonder bread, either. My mom put my sandwiches together using the big slices of roughly cut, homemade, whole-grain bread. She used the thick and chunky peanut butter we bought from the bulk bins at the health food co-op. And she didn't use jelly, just honey. I liked the taste, but the honey would ooze out all over the place and make a big mess. Sometimes my mom would put banana slices on the sandwich, too. I actually really liked to eat the sandwiches, but not in front of those school kids.

Being the sensitive little Pisces girl, worrying so much about what others thought of me, I could not bear to continue with the embarrassing lunchroom ridicule. Instead of eating openly in the line of fire of the insults, I hid in the girls' bathroom. I secretly ate my lunch in the privacy of a bathroom stall. I didn't always have time to finish my entire lunch because I was so nervous that someone would catch me. Many times I ended up throwing most of my lunch away in the trash.

I wonder how many of the kids who made fun of me grew up to be fanatical dieters with a gamut of health and weight problems. I often wonder if they even remember making fun of the little hippie kid in the lunchroom with her gross-looking healthy lunches as they huff and puff their way through their lunch-hour trip to the gym before grabbing a Big Mac and smoking a cigarette on their way back to work. Hopefully those kids grew up to become more aware than that. Perhaps they became vegetarians themselves. At the very least, many of them probably eat organic foods now. Some may even meditate and do yoga. Who knows? I survived the ridiculing of grade school lunch and hold no resentment towards those poor, ignorant children in the lunchroom of Central Elementary School in 1974.

"I Love you, God is Love, Om"

> I love you, God is Love.
> Om.
> Bless your blessing heart.
> Diamonds in your eyes, diamonds in the sky.
> Om.
> Singing through the green, green trees.
> Bless your blessing heart.
> Diamonds in your eyes, diamonds in the sky.
> Om.
> Singing through the blue, blue skies.
> Om.
> I love you, God is love.
> Om.
> *Lyrics to a song written by Ana at Mirkwood (age 6 or 7)

You just might be a hippie kid from the '70s if:

1. You got most of your clothes from a "free box" or from a thrift store.
2. Your clothes were mismatched and you owned one or more articles of tie-dyed clothing.
3. Your parents and most of their friends smoked pot. (Possibly you, too, smoked pot at a very young age.)
4. Your vegetarian diet consisted of a lot of sprouts, tofu, and organic fruits and veggies.
5. Your parents put brewer's yeast on your popcorn.
6. Your parents, or their friends, grew pot.
7. You lived without running water or electricity in a cabin, yurt, or tepee in the woods.
8. You lived on a hippie commune.
9. Your swimming excursions to rivers or lakes often occurred alongside skinny-dippers.
10. Your excursions to hot springs also involved soaking in the buff.
11. Your parents named you after a god, goddess, tree, or some other item in nature.
12. Your parents decorated with tapestries, an altar, and crystals, and had candles and incense burning at all times.
13. Your parents meditated and did yoga, and tried to encourage you to do the same.
14. Your medicines included Echinacea, goldenseal, and nasty-tasting herbal teas.
15. You saw an acupuncturist, naturopathic doctor, or chiropractor when you needed medical attention.

16. Your parents purchased all of your food at health food stores or co-ops, and mostly from bulk food bins.
17. Before every meal, your family held hands in a circle to give thanks for the food. They sang "grace," spoke a prayer, or simply sat with eyes closed in silence before eating. Perhaps everyone just simply "omed".
18. Your kitchen contained the main condiments of brewer's yeast, soy sauce, kelp powder, Braggs, and honey. You substituted chocolate with carob.
19. You bathed and washed dishes with Dr. Bronner's liquid peppermint oil soap.
20. You did not own a TV.

(Anastasia, 2008)

My friend Willow and me, 1976

Questions

❖

Growing up within the hippie culture definitely set me apart from normal kids my age. My entire being and outward appearance reflected the environment in which I was being raised. I felt a certain sense of innocence and naiveté about mainstream society and the world as a whole. However, I was very down to earth, observant, and aware of things that were going on in the immediate environment around me. On many issues about life I had already developed a sense of wisdom and understanding. Starting at an early age, I internalized many profound thoughts. I had so many unanswered questions.

What made me so different from the other kids in school? How I dressed? The food I ate? Was I the only kid to have ever been dosed on LSD? Perhaps the experiences I had already gone through in my seven-year lifespan set me apart. I had long hair, but most of the other girls at my school had long hair, too. I got most of my clothes from a thrift store or the "free box" outside of the New Frontier Market, a health food store in Eugene. My mom lovingly hand sewed all of my other clothes. I loved my homemade, hippie-girl peasant skirts with embroidered stitching on the trim. I thought my outfits were rather beautiful and fairy-like. "Normal" kids got their clothes from Sears or J. C. Penney, I guess. Hippie kids just had a certain look, which distinguished us from the rest of the world.

Possibly our parents' pot smoking set us apart. Or our healthy eating. Maybe it was our simpler lifestyle, free of consumerism. We weren't being brainwashed by the media of television. Ah, the sheltered life outside of mainstream society! That truly had a lot to do with our difference, I am sure.

I always had to answer difficult questions from other kids, their parents, my conservative relatives, and other adults who just didn't understand the hippie way of life. I faced questions like, "Why aren't you in school?" "What is that you're eating?" "Where do you live?" "Where did you get your clothes?" "Why can't you eat meat?" "What kind of name is Anastasia?" "How do you pronounce your name?" "What religion are you?" "Who is your dad?" "Why are you a vegetarian?"

The endless line of questions proved daunting and made me feel embarrassed at times. I'm sure many hippie kids endured the same feelings of being ridiculed with inquiries and having to justify how they lived. I was never sure how to answer all those questions. I definitely had to repeat myself a lot and explain how we lived, which didn't seem appropriate and somewhat of a burden for a child to have to endure.

The Oregon Country Fair

❀

J ust outside of Eugene, Oregon, hippies gathered every summer to experience the Oregon Country Fair (which continues to attract thousands of hippies and people from all walks of life today). I was six when I went to the Oregon Country Fair for the first time. Mirkwood had a booth set up to sell goods, and I worked as the sales clerk. We sold homemade clothes, handcrafted artifacts, baked goods, and smoothies. We made the smoothies using a blender rigged up to a stationary bicycle. Someone would mix up the smoothies by pedaling the bike to create the electricity to operate the blender.

I freely explored the fair on my own. I roamed with the other hippie kids, unsupervised. We made our way through the crowds of hippies to watch the circus and parades, and look at all the colorful characters, like the topless women with their breasts exposed for the world to see. We tried to figure out creative ways to make money of our own to buy things. My friends and I found rocks on the ground and drew little faces on them, which we sold for a quarter as "pet rocks".

People came from all over to the little town of Veneta, Oregon. The three-day fair happened in July every year and was the highlight of the summer for the hippies living in the Northwest. The fair became a tradition and a reunion, which I looked forward to each year throughout my childhood. The fair included such attractions as The Flying Karamazov Brothers, who juggled swords, flaming torches, and chainsaws; Reverend Chumleigh, with his magnificent magic act; and Moz Wright, the most impressive sword swallower of all time. These performers—along with the amazing food, rocking music, the strolling musicians, and Baby Gramps—were the highlight of the fair. Everywhere you went there were sounds of kazoos and laughter, drums, marimbas and jingling bells and cymbals from the belly dancers.

"Fair Time"

Musicians everywhere, jugglers, mimes and the hippie
circus!
Delicious food to eat, people with painted faces and no
shoes on their feet.
Sounds of laughter, hootin' and hollerin'!
Drum beats constant from the towers.
Stop at "The Ritz" for a sauna and a shower. Don't be
shy or shocked 'cause you're bound to see lots of bare
boobies, and cocks! Some even painted with flowers!
The trail is dusty, the sun is hot.
Hippies wandering around smoking lots of pot!
Contact high.
Scents of pennyroyal, patchouli, and lavender.
Cedar, sage, and incense fill the air. Experience, enjoy,
feel the love; it's all happening at the fair!

(Anastasia, 2009)

Food Issues

A standard, typical hippie diet doesn't exist. Many hippies are vegetarians and eat nothing but health food and food that is organically grown. Some hippies are strictly vegans, eating no animal products or byproducts whatsoever. A diet that includes fish and chicken but no red meat is very common amongst hippies as well. Plenty of hippies consume meat products and even dine on Big Macs at McDonald's. Realistically speaking, being a hippie has nothing to do with one's diet, even though hippies have been stereotyped in regards to their assumed diets. People commonly assume that all hippies are vegetarians and live on granola and tofu. I spent most of my childhood eating a strict vegetarian diet, with no meat whatsoever. No McDonald's. Only good, wholesome, organic, natural foods went into my body. My mom insisted on providing me with an all-natural, well-balanced diet.

For the most part, I didn't mind the limitations of the strict diet. However, it did make things somewhat challenging when

I would visit my friends and stay for dinner, or even visit with relatives at Thanksgiving.

I remember eating a hot dog one time at my friend's house when I was in first grade. I came home and told my mom about it. I didn't exactly get in trouble; I just got a lecture and felt really guilty. "It's your body!" my mom used to say to me. "One day you will thank me for forcing you to eat your sprouts, drink your carrot juice, and eat all your greens." Perhaps she had good intentions and believed she was doing the best thing for me. I always had food to eat, regardless of whether or not I liked the food. Little did I know that later on in life I would eventually face food issues, as do most other grown hippie kids, I am sure.

My issues became a matter of dietary choice and of identifying the acceptable foods for my body. Since I had always been ridiculed about the natural, whole foods I ate, and since I didn't care for the bitterness of raw sprouts, I developed an aversion to eating "healthy." But I also carried with me a guilty conscience about eating processed foods, sugar, meats, dairy products, prepackaged foods, and anything not organically grown.

The food issues I have dealt with my entire adult life have been very conflicting, to say the least. On one hand, eating healthy for me is associated with being ridiculed in grade school for eating such unusual food. On the other hand, processed food and the "normal" all-American diet have been proven to cause detrimental health effects. So, I have had to come to terms with maintaining a balanced diet and choosing to eat a relatively healthy combination of foods. I favor healthy eating and have an awareness of what I put into my body. I won't deny that I love bacon and Doritos. I have found out that moderation is the key. I have also learned that eating with guilt is not healthy.

Food issues for hippie kids varied. Some had to deal with strict diets which their parents enforced, not allowing them to eat certain foods such as meat and processed foods containing sugar. Others experienced painful neglect and went without eating at times. I have heard stories from some of my closest friends of how they would go for several days without having any meals prepared for them. They would have to fend for themselves and eat whatever they could find, if anything at all! Perhaps often eating something at a friend's house. Food was scarce for some families, especially, those living on food stamps and welfare. Some hippie parents would trade their food stamps for money to buy pot or other drugs instead of buying food for their kids. As far as I know, my mom never did that. She remained committed to providing me with the most wholesome, all-vegetarian diet, sprouts and all. In fact, my mom regularly fed other people's kids. She made sure that no one ever went without food.

Fairyland and Tepee Living

One of the most beautiful and magical regions of Oregon is the McKenzie River area. We spent about six months living near the McKenzie when I was nine. Still so innocent, I created a reality filled with fairies and elves. I could identify with the magical mystery of the woodland spirits. During the summer of 1977 we lived in a tepee in the woods set up on a beautiful piece of property near the town of McKenzie Bridge, an hour east of Eugene. Two other houses shared the property as well. The houses had electricity, running water, bathrooms, and flushing toilets. I enjoyed living in our tepee, especially since we had access to the "real" houses. I would often go to one of the houses to plug in my little turntable and play records. My favorite album at the time was The Beatles' *Abbey Road*.

This wasn't a "hippie commune," just a piece of land occupied by some of the people who had once lived at Mirkwood. Still, we lived the hippie lifestyle. My mom home schooled me during the fourth grade, which is the grade I would have been in if I had gone to school.

As for my home schooling experience, I would garden with my mom, write stories, and work math problems. My mom had studied wild herbs and their healing properties, sharing that information with me as well. I learned how to identify and collect a variety of wild plants. I kept a journal in which I pressed horsetail, chamomile, lavender, wild mint, comfrey, and other herbs from the garden. I labeled each plant sample, and I wrote some notes about their beneficial healing properties.

There were two other girls close to my age who lived nearby. They also had hippie parents. One of the girls lived in a tepee and the other girl's family lived in a converted school bus home. Together we would make up games to play in the woods. We created the most beautiful "fairy homes." At the base of a tree or in an old stump of a fallen tree, we would construct an entire housing complex for the fairies to inhabit. Using moss, sticks, flowers, branches, leaves, and rocks, we set up adorable little fairy homes. I truly believed in fairies and knew that after we went away, the fairies would come out and find the little homes we had built for them.

That summer I saw a solar eclipse, Elvis died, and I came in contact with my guardian angel. I had always known that she watched over me, but I had never given her a name. One afternoon, I sat outside of our tepee playing in the sun. I felt the presence of my guardian angel. I realized that I had no way to identify her, so I gave her the name Crescent. I had always been fascinated by, and in tune with, the phases of the moon. I liked the beautiful and magical crescent moon stage. So I decided to name my guardian angel Crescent, and continued to acknowledge her existence from that day on.

A tepee in McKenzie Bridge similar to the one we lived in
Photo taken by, Gary St. Martin

"Elf Story"

There once was a little elf. He was a smart elf. His name was Sunstar. He had many friends that lived with him in the big forest. His girlfriend's name was Moonflower. She lived a few trees down from him. Sunstar was kind of like the head of the forest because his father was king but had died. So Sunstar took over as the leader.

One day, Sunstar called a meeting to take place in the biggest tree, which was called the Meeting Tree. Everyone came from all directions, north, south, east, and west. They all got settled in the Meeting Tree. Sunstar said, "Why I bring this meeting together is because it is getting time to plant our gardens. We have to gather seeds and dry them so we can plant them in our gardens." Moonflower wanted to say something. She said, "I have a suggestion. We all should get dew-drop bags and each gather different kinds of seeds." Sunstar said, "That's a good idea. How does everyone feel about that?" Everyone yelled, "That's a good idea!"

Sunstar said, "Meeting out." Everyone went and got their dew-drop bags to gather all different kinds of seeds. They dried out the seeds and planted their happy little gardens. And they lived happily ever after.

The End.

* "Elf Story" written by, Ana
(Age 9)

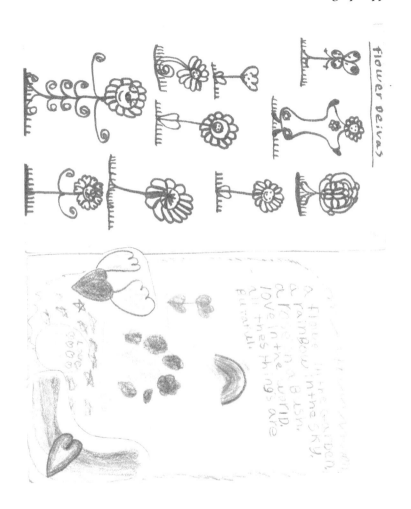

Art and poem by Ana, 1977

Cougar Hot Springs

❧

Cougar Hot Springs was about a 20-minute drive from McKenzie Bridge. Local hippies and travelers from afar enjoyed visiting the springs (and still do). It seemed everyone and anyone knew how to get there, which required an adventurous hike along the trail. Hiking in the woods, communing with nature, bathing in pools of hot water in the mud, and getting naked with a bunch of other hippies was a common pastime for lots of people. My mom and I visited Cougar hot springs often during my childhood. Every summer we would swim and play in the reservoir nearby. The rainy season made the paths muddy and slippery to walk on but we would still brave the elements and venture to the springs. We even sat in the springs in the wintertime with snow all over the ground.

Of course everyone bathed in the nude. It was natural, normal, and no big deal—the typical hippie thing to do. Everyone acted appropriately and respectfully toward each other (at least in my experience), though I realize that wasn't always the case for some. Even so, I maintained my modesty.

Once I reached puberty, I always wore my bathing suit, even though I had been raised around skinny-dipping hippies. Maybe it was my way of rebelling.

The hot spring pools lay deep in the woods surrounded by natural landscapes of fir, pine, and cedar trees, ferns, moss, bushes, logs, and stumps. The magic of the natural hot mineral water flowing out of the ground, filling up several pools, amazed me. The source of the spring bubbled out of a small little cave, filling a pool surrounded by rocks. The water from the upper pool trickled down filling the next pool below. Several pools cascaded down the side of the mountain. Since the water eventually cooled off the farther it flowed from the source, not many people sat in the lower pools. After soaking in the springs we would rinse off under the freezing cold, freshwater spring that was routed through a hose draped over a log. The showering off with cold water was part of the whole "spa" experience. The wet and muddy ground made it tricky to get dressed. But the cleansing, relaxing experience of the hot springs made it worth the hassle of being in the cold, wet, muddy conditions.

Spiritual Awareness

❦

The Sufi Invocation

Toward the One, the perfection of Love, Harmony and Beauty, the Only Being, united with all the Illuminated Souls, who form the embodiment of the Master, the Spirit of Guidance.

~Hazrat Inayat Khan

The hippie era brought with it the New Age of spiritualism. People became more aware, and concentrated on attaining enlightenment, as well as on developing a higher consciousness: becoming one with God; realizing that God is love; seeking the truth. Many people, both hippies or otherwise, focused on spiritual growth and expanding awareness. Throughout my childhood I was surrounded by a diversified group of spiritually minded individuals. My mom felt inspired to enrich her life through spirituality. Because of this, I too experienced the phenomenon of New Age, which prompted the desire for individuals to question organized religion and seek new methods of connecting with God. New Age followers practiced meditation, yoga, creative visualization, personal transformation, vision quests, oming, and chanting. The New Age movement enticed people in general, regardless of whether or not they were hippies. But hippies in particular became drawn to the movement and experienced spiritual awakening, especially during the '70s and '80s.

After several years of exploring and looking into a medley of religions, my mom found her spiritual calling within Sufism. Sufism is essentially Islamic mysticism. During the '60s, a man named Samuel Lewis became known as Murshid Sam started the first Sufi dancing meetings in San Francisco. Murshid Sam was a disciple of Pir-o-Murshid Hazrat Inayat Khan, who had brought the message of "Love, Harmony, and Beauty" over to the United States from India in the mid-1920s. Murshid Sam had tailored the teachings from a variety of traditions and world religions to a modern day approach, easily accepted and practiced by Americans, eventually expanding the teachings worldwide. He used Arabic prayers and sayings, along with a multitude of other world religions and traditions, setting them to music, and choreographed them with folk dance movements, thus creating Sufi dancing. "Dances of Universal Peace" is the current title used for Sufi dancing now.

The new Sufi movement appealed to a diverse crowd of people. The teachings about love, peace, and harmony made the studies acceptable and attainable by people from all walks of life, especially the hippies, whose whole belief system was based on these ideas. I believe that what appealed to those who became Sufis, is the fact that Sufism is not exactly a religion, but rather a way of a life. A spiritual life journey. Living each moment of your life with awareness and being thoughtful of everything around you with love and compassion for all beings. The teachings are passed on through a lineage from teacher to disciple through participation in group and private meditation practices, readings, prayer, song, and dance.

I was six years old when we first started to go Sufi dancing every Thursday night. It became my childhood tradition. I always looked forward to Thursdays. The group held dance meetings at the University of Oregon campus. Sufi dancing was fun! I always felt positive and happy after singing and participating in the dances. My inspiration and love for singing developed from those Thursday night dance meetings.

The upbeat, lively music filled the dances with energy. When we first started going to the dance meetings, I was the only kid there. After a while other kids started to participate with their parents. I met some of my best, lifelong friends there. I felt comforted knowing that other kids my age knew about Sufi dancing. I met two of my closest friends, Willow and Sage, while Sufi dancing. Their parents where hippies, too, and they also experienced commune living.

Smiling Forehead Sufi Center, Eugene OR. 1977
Photo taken by, Zehra Greenleaf

Arizona

❦

As my life's journey continued, my mother uprooted us once again. Somewhere between the ages of nine and ten, I moved to Arizona with her for a few months. Our travels brought us to Arizona so my mom could continue her studies on natural health and healing awareness. We attended a two-week health and healing conference with the leading pioneer of herbal medicine, Dr. John R. Christopher. I remember sitting through lectures and workshops on topics such as herbology, iridology, and healthy food awareness. As I sat through many of the classes with my mom, I found the topics to be very fascinating.

During one of the seminars, I had an iridology analysis done, which involved having a photo taken of my iris. I had slide photos taken of both of my eyes, which I carried around for a long time after that. An analyst read the various lines, marks, and colors on my iris. These readings can supposedly tell how healthy someone is and whether they have any prevalent health issues. As far as I can remember, I seemed to have had a clean bill of health.

After the healing conference finished, we had the opportunity to stay at a place called Healing Waters, located in a remote part of the desert near a town called Eden, halfway between Phoenix and Tuscan, Arizona. Hippies and New Age health experts ran the healing retreat center, offering healing gatherings, New Age awareness seminars, personal cleansing retreats, and natural food programs. But the best part about that place was the hot springs. At one time, the facility had been an actual resort, with an Olympic-sized swimming pool heated by the natural mineral hot springs, an old Victorian hotel, and several acres for camping.

My mom had the opportunity to study and work at Healing Waters, so we stayed there for a few months. Living in the desert was a completely new experience for me. I had always loved the sun, so the hot, dry heat was a nice change from the cold and rainy Northwest. Every day I swam in the natural hot springs pool and played with the other kids my age that also stayed there. I actually ran into one of my best friends from Oregon, Kathy, who was also staying there with her mom. Kathy and I always seemed to end up in similar places throughout our childhood since our parents moved around so much. We never planned or coordinated it, yet it seemed that the universe always brought us together at random places like healing gatherings, barter fairs, or at the Oregon Country Fair. It was always so exciting for me to run into Kathy at some unexpected time. We were such good friends and rarely had the chance to hang out and play together much since we were both always moving around to different places all the time.

My mom and I camped out in the desert the whole time we lived at Healing Waters, and we didn't even need a tent.

We set up our campsite with all of our belongings and arranged everything like a house, without walls or a roof. During the night, the sky grew really dark and as big as any I had ever seen before, since there were no trees or buildings to block the view. The nights were peaceful and a bit chilly. We went to the communal kitchen to eat all of our meals. Healing Waters always had some kind of seminar or gathering going on, and the meals served were prepared in accordance to the strictest of diets.

Visitors came to Healing Waters primarily to cleanse. The center offered a variety of all-natural, organic, vegetarian foods, including an assortment of completely raw foods. They offered every type of freshly squeezed juice, along with an array of sprouts—and not just alfalfa sprouts. Mung bean sprouts, sunflower sprouts, lentil sprouts, sprouted soybeans, sprouted wheatgrass—you name it, they sprouted it. Every morning they served freshly-squeezed orange and grapefruit juices, as well as cleansing drinks made from oranges, grapefruits, and lemons mixed with Cheyenne, garlic, and seaweed powder.

Most of the kids got tired of all the healthy food. We rebelled by getting someone to take us into town for pizza or Mexican food. Whenever we could, we raised money for the venture by selling fresh-squeezed orange juice and lemonade (which was funny, because those juices were offered as part of the program anyway). Even though it didn't happen very often, going to town and eating "real" food at a restaurant was a real treat!

Mysterious Rainbows in the Sky

One afternoon during a Healing Waters weekend retreat, everyone gathered on the front lawn of the hotel for lunch, making up a pretty large group of somewhere between fifty and sixty people. Kids played, climbing in the trees, running around. The adults sat around in groups, finishing up lunch, conversing, and preparing for the afternoon's activities. The sun shone brightly; the sky was a vivid deep blue, without a cloud in sight. I remember looking up into the sky after I noticed others around me looking upwards with astonished expressions on their faces. I remember having this feeling of disbelief and awe. A solid rainbow surrounded the sun. I had seen the sun have faint rainbows encircle it before, but not like this.

Directly off to the side of the sun, another rainbow appeared, but not in the typical arch that rainbows usually have; the shape was more of an eye. Three more images appeared, all in the same area of the sky overhead. As each image appeared, it was as if a paintbrush or a laser were "painting" the colorful images onto the canvas of the sky.

I could see no other objects, just the rainbow shapes. I can't exactly describe the shapes very well since they somewhat resembled hieroglyphic images. (I need to interject here that, to my knowledge, no one had partaken in hallucinogens at that time, and I know that I had not been dosed, either.) As the shapes appeared, they remained in the sky for several minutes before slowly fading away.

I still have found no explanation for the event that took place on that sunny afternoon in the middle of the Arizona desert during the fall of '77. Many assumed the phenomena was an act of aliens, or a form of communication from life forms other than humans. Maybe it was government experiments. In those days, pretty much all of the hippies believed in aliens. Many claimed to have had some kind of experience, sighting, or abduction. I really didn't know what to believe, but whatever happened was definitely out of this world and unusual.

My Grandma

❧❀❧

My absolute favorite person in the world was my grandma (my mom's mom). She was the family member I was the closest with and enjoyed visiting the most. She was a crack-up and always laughed really loud. Her laughter was infectious. I got to visit with her at least once, sometimes twice a year for a week or so each time. After hitchhiking from Oregon, or wherever we were living at the time, my mom would drop me off and go visit with her own friends in the Bay Area. My grandma was not a hippie herself, but she was very open-minded and accepting of everyone. She was spiritually minded, very loving and kind.

My grandma lived by herself in a modest one-bedroom apartment in San Mateo, California. I always thought she was rich and lived in a fancy place. From my perspective, she was. She always wore fancy dresses, high heels and lots of make up. She was very involved with the Methodist church, which I would attend with her on Sundays whenever I visited. After the service she would always proudly introduce me to all of her friends. This made me feel special. Almost like I was a celebrity or something.

Even though my grandma was very mainstream and lived somewhat of a conservative lifestyle she pursued spiritual growth and personal development. During the '70's she participated in EST (Erhard Seminars Training), which taught self-empowerment through a series of workshops and seminars. My grandma also studied *A Course in Miracles,* which teaches the concept of universal spiritual love and developing inner peace.

My grandma always seemed to be pursuing things in life towards becoming a better person. During one of my visits when I was twelve years old she was in charge of leading a discussion group at her church. The topic for the evening was based on a book called: *Love Is Letting Go Of Fear* by *Gerald Jampolsky.* My grandma asked me to assist her with the lecture. I helped by reading some of the excerpts from the book. The funny part about the event was that there was a misprint in the newspaper saying that Gerald Jampolsky himself was going to be there! We handled the situation with grace and humor. The participants who showed up, expecting to see the author, where all very understanding, once they realized the newspaper misprint. There was positive participation from the group, which consisted of about thirty people. After that evening my grandma gave me a copy of the book and signed it herself: " To Anastasia in remembrance of our stardom. With love, grandma."

Each visit to my grandma's was filled with non-stop fun. We would go out for lunch or dinner at fancy restaurants, shopping for clothes, go to the movie theater, and during the summer she would take me to Great America amusement park. We also frequently visited Marine World Animal Park and watched the whale shows. During my teen years my grandma and I would go to the symphony, or to watch a musical performance in San Francisco. I felt like royalty when we went into the city to see the San Francisco Ballet perform The Nutcracker.

Spending time with my grandma was some of the best times from my childhood. Being at her place felt comfortable to me and I could relax. I also knew that I could always count on her to be there for me. When it was time for me to leave I always cried. In fact, both my grandma and I would cry as we hugged each other good-bye. Tears streamed down both of our faces as we repeatedly hugged one another. Eventually I did have to break myself away and pull myself together. I really did not look forward to having to lug my backpack over my shoulders and head out on the freeway to hitchhike back to Oregon. Sometimes we rode the Greyhound or the Green Tortoise bus, which wasn't so bad. It was a difficult transition for me to go from having so much fun with my grandma to having to face the unknown. Sometimes we didn't even have a home to go back to. It was often a mysterious adventure, which I learned to accept by just going with the flow.

Vagabonds

~❀~

Hitchhiking takes a lot of patience, trust, tolerance, and a good sense of humor. We hitchhiked almost everywhere we went. My mom owned a car a couple of times, but mostly we got rides from friends or hitched out on the freeway. I found it difficult at times, and I complained a lot. We always got rides from nice people. Hippies commonly got around by hitchhiking. It was free; an adventure unhindered by the responsibilities of paying for gas, car insurance, or repairs. Sometimes we had to wait for hours to get a ride, sometimes overnight. One time in particular I remember being stuck on the side of the road with no one stopping to pick us up. It got so late, we ended up laying out our sleeping bags in the tall grass and sleeping on the side of the road.

I honestly cannot recall how many times during my childhood we hitchhiked from Eugene, Oregon, to see my grandma, and sometimes my dad, in California. We hitchhiked in the rain, the snow, and the scorching heat of summer. Sitting by the side of the road waiting for a ride was often agonizing, especially for a kid. It definitely took a lot of patience. Sometimes we got lucky and could get one ride most of the way to California. Sometimes it took several rides with hours of standing beside the freeway, waiting and waiting in the hot sun or the freezing cold rain as hundreds of cars whizzed by.

Big semis would stop for us on occasion and gave us rides, even though it was against the law. I especially liked riding in the big rigs. Truckers always treated us nicely, probably because most of them had families of their own back at home. I got so excited whenever we rode in one of those semis way up above everyone else, looking down on all the cars below. It was definitely an adventure. I remember having to hide in the sleeper cab when the trucks passed through the weigh stations because we didn't want to get caught. Truckers weren't supposed to have extra passengers, I guess.

For a short period of time, I had convinced myself that I wanted to be a truck driver when I grew up, mostly because of the experience I had riding in trucks and the adventures I could have traveling and seeing different parts of the country. (I think the movie *Smokey and the Bandit* had a bit to do with that, also.) Of course, my career choice quickly changed to acting, and I wanted to own a Trans Am when I grew up.

"Hitchhiking"

Scorching heat, bright sun, heavy backpacks.
Hard gravel, tired feet.
Fast cars zooming by.
Cars with lots of room.
Why won't they stop? The sun is hot.
They must think we're high on pot.
Show some compassion.
C'mon, we're just a pretty lady and her cute kid here
tryin' to get to our destination.

(Anastasia, 2009)

My Mom and me
Photo taken by Gary St. Martin

Eternal

I first encountered the Love Family in the summer of 1978 at the Oregon Rainbow Gathering. Rainbow Gatherings always brought people from all over the United States and abroad together for several days. (And still does!) In essence, it was one big hippie-fest, bringing people from all walks of life to unify and share the common vision of peace, love, and harmony throughout the planet. Each year, the gathering takes place in a different state, held on national forest land, open and welcome to everyone.

Families, whole communes, organizations (like the Hare Krishna), and individuals set up camps to create one large village. To some degree the Rainbow Gathering seemed the ideal place for groups and communes to recruit new members. For instance, the Hare Krishna always had an elaborate camp with a communal kitchen serving delicious food, with singing and chanting. I don't actually believe that The Hare Krishna are hippies, however, they always welcomed anyone, regardless of background, and lots of hippies joined their organization due to the spiritual support and inspiration.

The Love Family was a group of people who resided in Seattle, Washington. The Love Family camp included many kids, so I hung out with them. I met a girl who appeared to be around my age. She had been raised with the Love Family all of her life.

"How old are you?" I asked her.

She answered, "I'm eternal."

"A TURTLE?" I responded.

"No, ETERNAL," she said. She seemed pretty annoyed with me. Apparently the Love Family espoused the philosophy that everyone is eternal.

"Eternal? What the heck does that mean?" I asked. I was ten years old at the time.

The girl explained to me that we are all eternal. "Our souls have always existed, and they will exist for eternity." Wow! What a profound and sophisticated topic of conversation for two young children. That's hippie-kid mentality for you.

Intellectually, I completely understood the concept of being eternal. However, the cynical and sarcastic ten-year-old me persisted at trying to get the "eternal turtle" girl to tell me her real age. Frustrated by her, I was convinced that she would eventually give in and tell me how old she really was. I wanted a number, a birth date, something normal. I kept following this poor girl around calling her a turtle. She never did tell me her real age.

Washington and the Love Family

One year after I had harassed the "eternal" girl at the Oregon Rainbow Gathering, we went to live in Washington with the Love Family. I was eleven years old, *not* eternal. We arrived in Seattle just after going to a barter fair, yet another hippie gathering, where hippies all got together and camped in the woods for the weekend to trade or sell their arts and crafts. On Queen Anne Hill in Seattle, the Love Family operated a storefront/coffee shop/teahouse called The Front Door Inn. People would go here first to be introduced into the Family.

The Front Door Inn always served black tea with milk and honey, along with popcorn. A small bowl sat on the counter when you first walked through the door that contained little cards with virtues written on them. Guests could pick out a card at random and find a word to focus on for the day: peace, acceptance, openness, understanding, and many others. Tables and chairs, big pillows, and low tables filled the small establishment.

I will never forget the first night we arrived at the Love Family. It was customary for all visitors to be screened for head lice. After being examined, it was discovered that I had lice! More than likely, I had contracted them from the barter fair. Who knows? I remember feeling grossed out by the whole experience and a bit embarrassed. I was treated with the medicated shampoo, had all of my belongings washed and was rid of the lice.

Every morning at the crack of dawn, the Love family held morning meetings at the Front Door Inn. Family members would gather each day for a Bible study. I remember being very interested in the teachings of Jesus Christ; however, in my heart I knew that wasn't the only way to acknowledge God. My Sufi upbringing had already ingrained this in me. I did, however, attempt to read and familiarize myself with the Bible.

The neighborhood surrounding The Front Door Inn housed several households, each with an Elder who served as the head of the house. Elders had wives and children, with families, couples, and individuals all living communally within their households of about twelve people. Just north of Seattle in Arlington, Washington, the Love Family also owned a big ranch. The Ranch sat on a beautiful piece of property remotely located and surrounded by national forest land. Everyone lived in households there as well, except that the "houses" were enormous Army tents as big as small houses.

The Ranch did have one traditional main house, located at the entrance of the property. A gigantic barn served as the main gathering place. The ground level of the barn housed cows for milking (which I learned to do) and Belgium Clydesdale horses. The entire upper portion of the barn had been remodeled with impressive craftsmanship. The interior included all finished wood, windows with stained glass, and an industrial-sized kitchen with all the appliances to accommodate feasts for hundreds of people at a time. Bible studies, group meetings, festivals, musical performances, and feasts all took place in the barn.

Luckily, I didn't have a birthday during the time we lived with the Love Family—I wasn't too keen on the "eternal" concept. Family members typically gave up all their worldly possessions and cut off all ties to the outside world. They referred to anything outside the family as "the World." People who joined the family received a family name. Sometimes individuals would receive a Biblical name. A lot of folks had a "virtue" name like Understanding or Happiness. Other common names included Peace, Patience, Faith, Serious, Strength and Harmony. Everyone had the same last name: Israel. The founder and leader of the family had the name Love Israel. They never changed my name, maybe because Ana was already a Biblical name.

I remember having very few personal belongings, just my sleeping bag and some clothes. We lived a very simple and non-materialistic lifestyle. All of the women and girls wore dresses and skirts. Some of the men wore robes. Everyone had really long hair which they kept braided, and the men all had beards. Family members acted very peacefully and respectfully toward one another. Everyone involved with the family could have been considered a hippie by some standards. This group of individuals identified with and felt a strong connection to Jesus Christ. There was a common vision of creating a lifestyle by which to live. They had created a "tribe" and successfully followed their vision of living in harmony within a family. (In reality, I later figured out that it was more of a cult than the typical hippie commune.)

The family took schooling the children seriously also. They had a great home school program with qualified teachers. I really liked going to school there. They often held classes outside in the meadow on sunny days. They also used a little cabin for a schoolroom, as well as another building off the property to which the kids would get bussed. Overall, I enjoyed the experience of living with the Love Family, but a part of me felt relieved to move away from there because I had been cut off from the world. It felt good to be back in society and to interact with the rest of the world.

Christmas on the Road

One particular Christmas, when I was eleven years old, we actually had a car of our own to drive. My mom and I moved away from the Love Family and drove from Seattle down south through Eugene, Oregon, and then on to California. We left Eugene on Christmas Eve day. As we reached Ashland, close to the California border, our car broke down. It had already begun to get dark, and we ended up stranded by the side of the road. Snow surrounded us everywhere. Because it was Christmas Eve, no traffic passed by whatsoever. I remember being so disappointed and wishing so badly to be at my grandma's apartment in California.

After standing on the side of the road for what seemed like an eternity, hoping and waiting for a ride, we finally walked to a nearby hotel and got a room for the night. It was a rare treat for us to even stay in a hotel. Normally I would have been so excited and impressed by all of the luxuries and amenities: a TV, clean white sheets and towels, nice big beds high off the ground, and sparkling-clean bathroom fixtures. But on this night, the hotel room offered warmth and comfort from being stranded outside along the side of the road in the freezing-cold snow. I appreciated that comforting feeling more than the television set. I was too anxious to get on our way and finish the journey to my grandma's.

Waking up Christmas morning in a hotel room was pretty disappointing and uneventful. No tree. No presents. Not even a stocking from Santa. I think a part of me still believed and had a hopeful feeling that somehow, by magic, a stocking would be there for me. Instead we had to face hitch-hiking in the dreaded cold outside and continue our travels down the road to Grandma's. I managed to keep my spirits up and stay positive. Probably because of the excitement of it being Christmas and knowing we would eventually get to my grandma's, I was able to keep a feeling of giddiness and hope inside of me.

Very little traffic traveled along Interstate 5 on that Christmas day. Since we were unable to get our car repaired, we had to leave it beside the freeway and hitchhike. Even though it took the entire day to make the trip from Ashland to the San Francisco Bay Area, we finally made it. At one point we got a ride from a police officer. The cop picked us up and drove us as far as he could. I remember wishing he would just drive us all the way to my grandma's, but he didn't. We also got a ride in a semi that had been delivering candy canes. The driver took us all the way to the front of my grandma's apartment building.

We arrived late in the evening of Christmas day. My grandma was anxiously waiting for us to arrive. When we pulled up to her apartment building in the giant semi, I remember seeing my grandma standing on the sidewalk waving her arms and smiling. I climbed out of the big rig and ran into her arms. We hugged each other so tight. I don't think I had ever been so happy to see my grandma more than at that moment. It was such a relief to finally be done with such a long day of hitchhiking. Especially with it being Christmas day! We celebrated Christmas that night with presents and a delicious home made dinner.

Homeless

❧

H ome really is where the heart is. Moving from place to place, not staying very long and changing schools often, I adapted the best that I could. In some ways my childhood of instability caused me to become flexible and unattached. I developed a real "go with the flow" attitude. Most of the time, I had to leave personal possessions behind when we moved. I found it difficult to part with my belongings, like toys, books, knickknacks, and treasures I had collected. For the most part, I could only bring with me what I could carry: a duffle bag or backpack with my clothes, a sleeping bag, stuffed animals, a book or two to read, and art supplies. I also could pack a few treasures, trinkets, jewelry, and special little items such as gifts I may have received from my grandma.

I also hated leaving friends behind. The friendships I had developed as a child always seemed to withstand all our moving around. I ran into friends during our travels because their parents were traveling hippies, too. We all seemed to travel the same circuit of Rainbow Gatherings, barter fairs, and Sufi camps, and visited some of the same places. Other friends remained in the Eugene area and were always there whenever we returned, friends like Willow and Sage. I always looked forward to going back to Eugene because of them.

Even though we transitioned a lot and moved frequently during my childhood, I managed to find some continuity and structure within our many journeys. I always looked forward to Thursday night Sufi dancing, the Saturday market in Eugene, the Oregon Country Fair, and Sufi camps. In July, we always traveled to California for the Mendocino Sufi camp, and then returned to Oregon in August for the Northwest Sufi camp at Breitenbush hot springs. These events gave me a feeling of comfort and stability, something to rely on, and provided positive experiences filled with fun times and good people who were like family to me.

More often than not whenever we traveled someplace, we didn't necessarily have a home to return to. Sometimes we would stay with friends, rent a room in a shared house, or live in our car (if we had one), or of course, stay at one of the many hippie communes we visited.

When I was twelve, my mom had a boyfriend who had an old Chevy van painted green with a VW bug welded to the roof. For about a month we lived in the van parked along the streets of Seattle. What an adventure that was—talk about close quarters and no privacy! We stayed out in front of our friend's house, which gave us a place to take showers and prepare food. Eventually we moved our van home over to the San Juan Islands to Orcas Island. We lived on the island for about a month with some friends of ours who had a big house close to the beach.

A lot of hippie families lived in various situations in those days. Many were homeless, living wherever they could. Some lived in trailers, apartments, or houses in the city. Others lived in communes out in the country, or in custom-built cabins with elaborate architectural details. It probably depended on how much income they had and what kind of lifestyle they preferred.

As I reflect back on being homeless, I can honestly say that it was not all that bad. I always felt safe, had plenty of food to eat, and knew that my mom loved me and took good care of me. I also had the comfort of knowing that I had my guardian angel looking out for me. I accepted our homelessness as the hippie way of life, part of the whole hippie kid experience. Of course I won't deny the inherent desire to have had a normal, stable, single-home way of life. But my life is what it is. My experiences made me who I am.

More Adventures and Survival

Around the time I was twelve and a half we lived with a group of hippies who had just started up a commune named Antankarana Circle in the mountains of northern Washington, three miles from the Canadian border. It was another classic "live off the land" situation. Everyone contributed to the community in order to become self-sustaining. I felt challenged by this experience, because at the age of twelve and a half I really wanted to be living in civilization with electricity, running water, and the comforts of a normal lifestyle like going to school, watching TV, and having friends my age to interact with. Instead, I once again found myself completely isolated and forced to learn basic survival skills. It turned out to be another exciting adventure in my history.

That winter my mom and I lived with her new boyfriend in a tepee. Oh, how awkward that was, especially when they had sex! Yes, most hippie kids who lived in small dwellings like a tepee, cabin, or a bus either listened to or witnessed their parents "getting it on." It snowed that winter in

113

Washington; thank God we had a woodstove in our tepee to keep us warm and to cook. The tepee itself was set up on a large wooden deck in the middle of a meadow on the side of a hill. Down the hill a little ways ran a stream where we got water for washing and drinking. Once the coldest part of winter hit, the stream froze over. We had to break away the ice to get to what little water flowed through. We could then fill the buckets and carry them back up the hill to our tepee.

The commune had one outdoor shower for bathing. We heated the water in a big metal barrel over a fire pit, and would have to keep the fire going for a long time in order to heat enough for a shower. Since the shower sat outside, it would get freezing cold once the hot water ran out, and then showering time would end. Then we would stand next to the fire to stay warm while we got dressed. This could be rather awkward since we had little privacy and stood out in the open.

I made the best of the winter months. A marsh on the land would freeze over, making it the perfect winter wonderland to play on. My grandma had given me a pair of ice skates, which I could finally use. Exploring the frozen environment of the marsh proved to be an adventure. Beaver dams, trees, logs, and various bushes and grasses poked out of the ice. I skated all over the place. I had always loved roller-skating, but skating on the ice was nothing like being inside at the roller derby.

Earlier that fall, when we first moved onto the land, I met a girl close to my age named Feather. She used to come out to the land with her parents and visit with us. Her family had a bunch of horses, which they would bring to the barter fairs. We attended the barter fair in Washington that year in a remote part of national forest land. (National forest land seemed to be the common place to hold large gatherings of hippies.)

People came from all over to camp out and set up booths to trade crafts, tools, food, produce (particularly apples), and other homemade goods. People camped in tents, buses, tepees, cars, RVs, tarps, domes, and yurts. Campers enjoyed campfires where people sang and played music together, visited food booths and shared communal kitchens while the kids ran everywhere playing. It reminded me of a Rainbow Gathering with fewer people and the ability to drive right up to the campsite with no long hike.

During that barter fair, I hung out with Feather and rode her horses. After the barter fair, we asked if we could ride two of the horses down the mountain and meet up with her family at a certain point before the back roads joined the highway. We prepared for our ride and said our good-byes.

We set out early in the morning on our adventure. The sun shone; it was a beautiful day for a ride. I had plenty of experience horseback riding because one of my best friends in Oregon had horses, and I used to ride with her every summer. We took an unpaved Forest Service road, which took us down the mountain through miles of forests. We rode for several hours and never once saw a car. I recall that we stopped at times to let the horses rest and get a drink from a river or a spring. At some point we figured that we had gotten lost because the road went on endlessly and never seemed to meet up with any other roads. It grew late in the day when we finally reached a paved road. Neither one of us felt worried or scared at all. When darkness set in, we became tired and somewhat concerned also knowing that we needed to stop someplace and rest. I think we both knew that we would be fine and that our families and others would come looking for us.

By nightfall, we started to pass farms with houses. Eventually we came upon a house close to the road with lights on inside and a corral with a horse right next to it. We both had a good feeling about the place. We got off our horses, went up to the door of the house, and knocked. A nice young guy answered the door. He had just finished dinner and was visiting with some friends. We told them our story, and he welcomed us in to stay for the night. He put the horses into the corral, which could be seen clearly from the road, and my friend and I slept safely for the night. We shared the couch and managed to get a good night's sleep.

Very early the following morning, we woke to knocking on the door. One of our parent's friends had found us. He told us that various people looked for us throughout the night. He found us because of the horses, which he could see from the road. Once again, I felt blessed and protected by my guardian angel, and fortunate to have stayed positive and brave. We enjoyed the adventure and trusted in the Great Spirit that we would stay safe and find our way home. And thanks to that unknown stranger who took us in and treated us with respect and kindness, we had a safe place to stay for the night.

Culture

❦

From my observations and experiences growing up within the hippie culture, I have concluded that the hippies derived a myriad of traditions from all over the world, likely creating one of the most diverse subcultures in history. Hippies based the very foundation of their principles, beliefs, and way of life on peace and love. Because many cultures worldwide practice and believe in peace and love, several different cultures seemed to have influenced setting the tone for the whole hippie way of life.

By combining a hodgepodge of traditions, the hippies created a colorful way of living. Meditation, spiritual practices, music, and philosophies came from all over the world, including India and Asia, the countries of South America, the Gypsies of Eastern Europe, many tribes of Africa, and the Middle East. Native American culture also made a big impact on the hippies. Hippies incorporated many Native American traditions into their lifestyle. Jamaican Rastafarian culture most likely held the biggest influence on the collective consciousness surrounding the sacredness of smoking marijuana.

The hippie lifestyle was truly a unique and eclectic way to live; from traveling in caravans and performing like Gypsies, to practicing yoga and meditation like the peoples of India, to following the ancient healing arts of the Asian culture and performing ceremonial traditions adopted from the Native American peoples. Perhaps there are many other cultures to give recognition to as well, but from my observation and experience, those are the ones that stand out the most.

Sufi Summer Camp

I spent every summer, from the time I turned seven until I turned seventeen, attending Sufi camps. I enjoyed the program for children, which included arts and crafts, music, singing, dancing, nature walks, and talent shows performed for the rest of the camp. We sang songs and did Dances of Universal Peace. Camp leaders also taught an introduction to spiritual teachings at age-appropriate levels. I always had a great time and made lots of friends. My mom would often work as a cook in the kitchen or as a teacher for the kids' camp in exchange for our camp tuition.

During my teen years I participated in the main camp activities with the adults, such as classes in spirituality, music, dance, meditation, healing, women's studies, astrological and elemental "walks" practices, and of course, Sufi dancing. I enjoyed participating in all of the classes. At mealtimes, we ate delicious gourmet vegetarian meals and spent fun social time visiting and hanging out with the other campers. Every evening included an amazing program such as a musical performance, Sufi dancing, and toward the end of camp, a talent show and choir performances. Some nights also included a zikr.

At a zikr, everyone sings the name of God (traditionally in Arabic) repeatedly through various harmonies and melodies. Simple dance movements go along with the music, as instructed by a teacher. In a way it resembles the Dances of Universal Peace, only with more repetition and simpler movements. It can be both energizing and intense as well, especially since phrases are repeated over and over again.

My favorite classes included singing with the choir and the "walks" class. The "walks" class provided instruction on concentration and awareness of being, and how to walk with a purpose. The practice concentrates on different planetary and astrological characteristics, as well as the elements of earth, water, fire, and air, which helps individuals become aware of how to walk with intention by focusing on a specific concentration.

Summers at Sufi camp resembled other church camps except for the New Agers and the alternative crowd. Lots of hippies attended, but the camps attracted more mainstream types as well. It was always a nice combination of folks from all walks of life. I always looked forward to going every summer.

On the last Sunday of camp, participants gathered for the universal worship service. This amazingly beautiful service honored religions and traditions from all over the planet, often outside in a meadow or indoors at an altar arranged with candles and flowers, incense and pictures. Lit candles represented each tradition, honoring the God or deity recognized for that particular religion. As participants lit each candle during the service, a reader presented a short excerpt from the manuscript or book of that particular tradition (the Bible for Christianity, for example). A song or dance followed the reading. Prayers and Dances of Universal Peace also contributed to the service. Essentially, universal worship was "hippie church," honoring multiple religions in a unique way.

I had one of the most memorable times at any Sufi camp the summer after I turned thirteen. I brought my best friend, Darcy, with me to the Northwest Sufi camp at Breitenbush Hot Springs Retreat Center. Darcy wasn't really a hippie at all. She lived in Los Angeles and came up to Oregon to visit her dad every summer. We had so much fun that summer attending the classes, singing with the choir and performing in a pageant and dance performance for the entire camp. We swam in the river and soaked in the hot springs, aside from participating in all of the camp activities.

The highlight of the camp for me that year was participating in the women's studies class. The class focused on honoring women from all different traditions throughout history. We learned dances, sang songs, meditated, and created rituals. We held a ceremony honoring the four phases of a women's life: the young maiden entering womanhood; a woman preparing for marriage; a pregnant woman preparing to give birth; and an elder woman passing through menopause.

In this beautiful ceremony, I represented the young maiden entering womanhood, a very sacred event about to take place in my life. Before the ceremony, I was asked to choose four different women to represent the four directions and to serve as my "guides." These women would be strong female role models who would always be there for me.

The four women I chose included my mom, Mariam, Hilal, and Deborah, all of whom I had a bond with since early childhood.

The ceremony was very sweet. I felt a sense of importance and a feeling of support and encouragement as I stood in the center of three circles of women surrounding me. The setting evoked a sense of magic. The large, open room had windows all around that looked out into the forest surrounding the building. Sunlight streamed in, filling the room with light. My four guides stood around me in each of the four directions, and each presented me with a gift and heartfelt words of wisdom. We exchanged hugs, as they gave me blessings to welcome me into the realms of womanhood. I felt honored. The ceremony was definitely a significant event in my life, full of light and inspiration.

Whirling Dervishes

~❀~

Come, come, whoever you are. Wanderer, worshipper, lover of leaving. It doesn't matter. Ours is not a caravan of despair. Come, even if you have broken your vows a thousand times. Come, yet again, come, come.

~Rumi

*A*n opportunity arose for my mom to study the art form of whirling Dervishes with a teacher from Turkey named Jelaluddin Loras. In order to receive firsthand teachings of the whirling Dervish forms, we moved to San Rafael, California, for six months. Marin County, California, was a much more progressive and fascinating place to be for a teenager than all the other places I had ever lived. I had just turned fourteen. I didn't mind leaving Oregon behind once again. We weren't moving to some remote, dropped-out hippie commune in the woods this time. We were moving to the big city!

We lived in a communal household with a bunch of Bay Area Sufis. The house, called Sami Mahal had three levels, nine bedrooms, three bathrooms, and a large wrap-around porch. It sat on a hillside overlooking the city of San Rafael. We had ten roommates. Everyone living there had professional jobs and mostly commuted into San Francisco for work. Everyone took turns preparing meals, cleaning the house, shopping, and washing dishes.

Most of the folks who lived at Sami Mahal were, at one time, hippies. Even though most of them may have had hippie beliefs and philosophies, they didn't resemble the majority of Oregon hippies I had known. It could have been the difference between "city hippies" and "country hippies." Also, in the early eighties, many people who lived an experimental hippie life in their younger years had evolved into "yuppies."

My mom began whirling Dervish studies with Jelaluddin Loras, who also lived at Sami Mahal. I, too, began attending classes twice a week, which we held in the large open living room at our house for a while. That room had hardwood floors and stayed empty to accommodate the variety of dance, music, and meditation classes taught there. A weekly zikr held on Thursday nights was also held there as well. When more people started to attend the whirling Dervish meetings, the classes were moved to a larger facility.

For the discipline, focus, and style of dance meditation, I found the art of the whirling Dervish studies fairly interesting. I enjoyed being a part of a group practice. The first year that we participated, I was the youngest participant. The following year, one of my best friends, Jessica also joined the group and learned how to "turn".

By day, I went to the local middle school, finishing eighth grade. In the evenings, I attended whirling Dervish practice. Not volleyball or cheerleading: whirling Dervish. Participants were referred to as "Semazens". The classes led up to a performance in December called Sema or Sebi-Arus. Every year on December 17 the Dervishes traditionally perform the ritual of whirling to celebrate the "wedding day" which is the day of Mevlana Jelaluddin Rumi's passing.

After we moved away from San Rafael, my mom and I continued to practice "turning" on our own and went back to attend rehearsals. Each December we would return to the Bay Area so that we could participate in the Sema. I participated in the annual performance of the Sema until I turned 17 years old.

Mendocino

I found the term "high school" appropriate because for the first three years of it, I was high. My mom found out about a great alternative high school in Mendocino, California, called The Community School. Most of the students had hippie parents. I had finally found a school where I fit in perfectly! The students created their own schedules, attended small classes, and often worked independently by themselves or in small groups without a teacher. The Community School had music studios, a computer lab, various classrooms, and a greenhouse for horticulture studies. Students could also receive credit for projects and activities completed outside of school. The school awarded me credits for participating in the whirling Dervish classes, for example (for which we still regularly commuted back to San Rafael).

Every morning, school started in the main library with a morning meeting. Teachers, students, and some parents gathered in a big circle to discuss different issues, goals, and important events. After the meeting, all of the students went to their classes or independent studies, or to work on projects or practice music. The school sat on the edge of town, near the cliffs overlooking the Pacific Ocean. Trees surrounded the school in its beautiful setting just a short walk from the beach.

Music inspired me. I sang with the choir, took private voice lessons, and tried to learn the piano, but singing was my passion. A bunch of kids had formed bands of their own. This was the early '80s, and many hippie kids were into heavy metal. Most of the cutest guys at the school were in a rock band, or at least played an instrument. My girlfriends and I hung out in the music studio and listed to the guys practice music.

I had my first high school crush on a boy named Chris Fox. He was the hottest drummer in the school and he could actually play the drums too. We never dated as boyfriend and girlfriend, but we did make out on occasion. He kissed pretty well, and since I had never kissed a boy before, he taught me how to kiss, too. It was kind of like a real-life sex Ed class. We would go down to the beach, fool around, and make out without actually having sex. I'm sure most of the kids who went to the school explored all kinds of things like that on their own, trying to figure out life through sex, drugs, and rock and roll, following in their hippie-parents' footsteps.

The Community School did not keep strict attendance, probably in an effort to develop trust and let the students learn to be responsible for their own actions. Of course, hippies ran the experimental school with hippie values and beliefs. I acted responsibly as I could and made sure to get my work done, however socializing was my favorite activity during my freshmen year. My friends and I would leave school during lunch and walk around the town of Mendocino. We used to go out for coffee almost every day. The quaint coffee houses in Mendocino had the best fresh-ground coffee I had ever tasted, starting my life-long love for fresh-ground coffee. I blame it on the excellent coffee served at the Café Beaujolais. After drinking coffee and eating lunch someplace like the Main Street Deli, my friends and I would walk up the hill to the graveyard to go "smoke out." It seemed that every kid who went to The Community School smoked pot.

At the beginning of the school year I rarely smoked pot, given my early childhood exposure to pot and other drugs. But internally, I battled going down that road. Here I was, at that turning point in my life, where nature takes the course of rebellion in some form or another. In a strange way, I had been rebelling for most of my life, trying to fit in with the "straight" world. Now I had found myself among a group of peers with similar upbringings who also smoked pot. Partly for the social experience and partly for their acceptance of me, I took up with the crowd of pot smokers, and I made the greatest friends. I felt comfortable and I could be myself. Surrounded by a group of peers I could identify with so closely enabled me to transition through puberty with ease. I felt accepted for the first time in a school setting, and I didn't feel judged for being a hippie kid.

During our first month of living in the Mendocino area, we lived in our car and stayed with friends. We managed to find a place to live for a month in a little camper trailer on someone's property. Many of the "Community Schoolers" floated around, not actually living in a permanent home. Some stayed with friends and didn't even live with their parents. My mom and I eventually rented a house with a deck that overlooked the ocean. I slept in the only bedroom, while my mom slept out in the living room. We didn't have a TV, but we did have a telephone, and the place came furnished, so I had a real bed to sleep in. We only lived in that house for a few months before moving to a little trailer on my best friend's property.

During the spring of my freshman year my mom decided that we would move back to Oregon. I wanted to finish off the school year before moving. I didn't want to leave my friends behind. I was sick of leaving so many friends behind and never finishing an entire school year. After discussing all the details with my mom I was able to convince her to let me stay. My mom arranged for me to live with my best friend Sherry and her family while she moved back to Eugene. Thus I joined the majority of the student population at my school who was left on their own, to discover independence for themselves. I wasn't exactly left on my own though since I did have Sherry's parents looking out for me.

During the summer just before I moved away from Mendocino, I voluntarily took acid for the first time since being dosed as a young child. Sherry and I tripped the entire day walking out in the woods together. I don't recall having any significant hallucinations or impressions from the experience. That summer I also tried cocaine for the first time which was not a good feeling at all. I remember feeling extremely energized and full of anxious energy. After that experience I remember thinking to myself that I would just stick with only smoking pot. On the first weekend of summer vacation I went to my first "kegger" (a party with kegs of beer), where I drank for the first time, too. It didn't take much for me to feel "tipsy". I kind of liked the feeling from the "beer buzz".

I definitely gained a sense of independence during that year of living in Mendocino. I also learned many real-life lessons. Moving away from Mendocino proved one of the most difficult moves for me because I had made so many good friends. I had also finally found a place where I could really be myself in a school setting.

My friend Jessica and me, Teenage hippie girls!

Eugene Again...

❀

Having spent so many years living in and around the Eugene area, it felt familiar and comforting to move back to Oregon. However, starting a new school once again felt anything but comforting. It took me a few months until I finally found the cool kids to hang out with. Being in a new school, surrounded by "normal" kids once again made me feel insecure and out of place.

South Eugene High enrolled eighteen hundred students, unlike the small, intimate school full of hippie kids I had attended in Mendocino. At South there were so many different social circles and categories to fit into. The smart, clean-cut kids hung with the preps. Then there were the sporty jocks. We called the popular kids the socies, and of course we had the typical nerds as well. We referred to the kids who rode skateboards as the skaters, and the punk-rock crowd as the punkers. When I discovered the rockers and the stoners, I knew I had found the social circles where I fit in best—with the "bad" kids who skipped classes to smoke pot and cigarettes. I didn't smoke cigarettes myself, but I did try smoking "cloves" occasionally. Those were really strong clove cigarettes that became popular for a while.

Music remained my passion. I loved to sing. Between singing with the school choir and hanging with my social circle, I looked forward to going to school every day. Here, my internal battle continued, the battle I have always faced between feeling comfortable and feeling different. Somehow I found a balance between taking school seriously, fitting in, and still having fun with the social scene where I felt most comfortable. Still, I felt awkward, like I lived a double life. I had my close friends, the stoners with hippie parents. Those friends could all relate to living the same lifestyle I had. I also had my more conservative friends from my choir and drama classes. During the school day I really tried to appear normal. I dressed conservatively, attempted to get good grades, attended classes, and followed the school rules. I didn't want to stand out as being different. I didn't want the bad reputation from the teachers of a stoner. Even though I did attend class high at times, I did a good job of covering it up. (At least I think I did.)

This all changed after school and on the weekends. I could relax, party, and be myself with my friends. I smoked pot, took acid, and listened to Pink Floyd, Jimi Hendrix, the Grateful Dead, the Rolling Stones, Led Zeppelin, AC/DC, Ozzy, the Scorpions, and Van Halen. I would hang out with my friends for hours talking, listening to music, doing artwork, and just laughing our asses off. If I put a label on myself, I would have been a stoner/rocker chick, the natural evolution for some hippie kids becoming teens in the '80s.

Trippy doodle art I did in High school, 1985

On some weekends, I would baby-sit for my mom's friends. I loved doing that because they would pay me well and leave me buds to smoke, an added bonus to babysitting for pot growers or dealers. If I babysat on Friday or Saturday nights, I could sit back, smoke pot, and watch TV while the kids slept.

My mom worked as a massage therapist healer, and her boyfriend worked as an acupuncturist. They worked together in an office in downtown Eugene. We lived in the southwest hills of Eugene, in a quiet neighborhood on a dead-end street surrounded by an undeveloped area. A bit of forest surrounded our house, yet we still lived within the city limits. My mom had a huge garden where she grew organic veggies. For the first time, we lived in a real house with no roommates or communal living situation. It felt permanent, not just a temporary place to stay before moving on. I even had my own room, which gave me the opportunity to acquire more personal possessions beyond what would fit inside of a backpack.

During my high school years, we started to incorporate meat into our diets. Mostly we would eat fish, chicken, and turkey. We even had KFC on occasion. For the first time in my life I felt stable and secure. We lived in the same house for four years, the longest we had ever stayed in one place. My mom had her own car and we never hitchhiked again. I actually felt normal. My friends thought my mom was the coolest mom ever. Actually, I did, too.

During the mid-'80s some hippies living in urban areas gradually evolved into "yuppies". My mom managed to incorporate the values and beliefs of the hippie culture into living a more mainstream lifestyle. Most obviously, she dressed more conservatively, maintained a professional job, and drove a new car. We even owned a TV and had a telephone.

Cynicism

❧

E ugene, Oregon, has always had a reputation for being a hippie Mecca. It boasts the Oregon Country Fair, a variety of health food stores and co-ops, support of local artists and musicians, alternative energy sources, organic farming, and liberal thinking. The full spectrum of hippie life surrounded me, from hard-core, radical protesting types, to mild-mannered, airy-fairy, soft-spoken types, to the presumptuous and pseudo-wannabes. I have learned through experience and observation that hippies don't follow a prototype. People are people. Being a hippie is just another way of life that each individual interprets differently and expresses uniquely.

Somewhere along the line, I developed a cynical view of the hippies around me. I became judgmental, especially towards those who expressed an arrogance or righteousness about their hippie personas. That always seemed to bug me. Even though I knew better, and was taught to love and accept people for who they are, I still developed a bit of a cynical attitude towards some of the hippie culture over time. It takes a lot of self-control to always keep an open mind and not judge the ignorance of others.

"Cynical Hippie Kid"

You say far out. I say way in. Right on, how about
left off?
Can you dig it, or do you need a shovel?
Who are you to think you are so cool?
Perhaps your dyes are tied too tight.
The reflection in your eyes, is it too bright?
The harshness of reality, is it too much to handle?
Sit back, relax and focus on a candle.

(Anastasia, 2008)

"Too Groovy"

Sparkling eyes, glowing aura. Radiance.
Feeling colors, seeing sounds, tasting
laughter. Drinking life.
The hunger to know. But Why? How did we
get here? Where do we go when we die?
To dwell on a thought. Be in the moment.
Live for today. Love. The universe provides.
We are all one. Peace, Love, Joy,
and tofu for all!

(Anastasia, 2008)

Hippies are everywhere! They come from all walks of life!

- Country Hippies
- Redneck Hippies
- Tree-hugger Hippies

- City Hippies
- Gun-toting Hippies
- New Age, Spiritual Hippies
- Health-Food Fanatical Hippies
- Rich Hippies
- Poor hippies
- Dirt-Poor Hippies
- Homeless Hippies
- Hard-Working Hippies
- Good-Hearted Hippies
- Radical Hippies
- Con Artist Hippies
- Wannabe Hippies
- Generous Hippies
- Prejudice Hippies
- Ego-tripper Hippies
- Trippy Hippies
- Airy-Fairy Hippies
- Free-Loader Hippies
- Rainbow Hippies
- Hollywood Hippies
- Proud Hippies
- Righteous Hippies
- Crazy Hippies
- Wandering Hippies
- Dirty Hippies
- Freaky Hippies
- Hippie Dippies
- Lazy Hippies
- Aggressive Hippies

- Educated Hippies
- Fanatical Hippies
- Misunderstood Hippies
- Aware Hippies
- Lost Hippies

California Rainbow Gathering

~❀~

(My diary/journal entry after returning from the California Rainbow Gathering when I was sixteen years old.)

July 15, 1984

My mom, Suzi, (who is my best friend) and I drove to the Gathering together. We had a good time. When we first got there (to the gathering sight) we found a camp for the teens called "Barbaria," Teen Village. Suzi and I both thought of "Guys!" so we went and checked it out. Right away we met this good-looking guy who was 16. Other teens were there too, only they were younger. We decided to camp there. Three guys helped us put up our tent. Suzi and I played "dumb" like we didn't know how to set up the tent. Everything went great the first day. One of the teenage boys taught me how to play Hackey Sac. It was great to finally learn how. The second day, Suzi and I each took a half hit of 'cid and we didn't tell anyone except for my mom and this one guy, Dale, (aka Peaceful Valley Walker) who was 19. He kept coming up to us and telling us, "It sure is good to see so many smiling faces around here." Suzi and I would just burst out laughing. Nobody else knew. I had a good trip. So many good things happened. Every time I looked at that cute guy Dale, I would smile and I felt good. Well, the next day we all hung out together at "Barbaria" (teen village). There were so many nice people there. There was another 16-year-old girl there too. She lives in New York. There were around 17 teens total all camped out in Teen Village. We got high together and the kitchen trip was really together. One night we all made chicken and spaghetti. Suzi got "burned out" on the gathering so she got a ride home early. Thursday night I hung out with all of my new friends (in the teen communal tepee). I kept looking at Dale, the cute guy. Every time I would look at him, he would already be looking at me! There was so much energy between our eyes when they met. Finally, after most of the night watching each other, we sat next to each other and I was leaning against him as a backrest. Our energies seemed to connect somehow. He said that I had "a nice aura." (End of diary entry.)

As for the rest of the Gathering, Dale and I hung out together the whole time. We had an innocent, young-hippie romance based on kissing, gazing into each other's eyes, holding hands, and talking. We formed a good connection on a heart level, where we enjoyed being in each other's presence. After the gathering, we brought Dale home with us. He had planned to hitchhike around the West Coast anyway, and wanted to check out Eugene. He slept out on our screened porch for a couple of nights and then went off on his merry hippie way. It wasn't like we were boyfriend and girlfriend—in fact, once we left the gathering sight, my interest in him as anything other than a friend had vanished. The magic of an innocent, young romance—of being lost in the moment—had blinded me temporarily. Thank God Dale didn't push me or expect anything from me, because I wasn't about to lose my virginity to some random, good-looking, hippie traveler from a Rainbow Gathering! That California Rainbow Gathering was the last gathering I ever attended.

"After-Hours Teenage Country Fair Tripper"

Nighttime at the fair—there's real magic in the air.
The mystery unfolds before your eyes, as the elfin
spirits come alive!
Sparkles, laughter, smiles, and giggling fairies delight.
Fire dancing, flames juggling, fire breathing dragons.
Dragons? Man? Dragon. No it's a man, relax, it's
just the acid.
Tracers from glow sticks stream through the air.
The pizza booth is still open, ooooh yum. Want some?
Saucy, cheesy pizza hits the spot.
Now it's time to go toke some pot.
Watch the midnight show, the crowd is too trippy…
One big rolling wave of laughter coming out of all
those silly hippies.
I'm just a speck absorbed in the sparkles of the stars above.
Zoning, drifting, laughing, floating.
Trip on back to camp. Relax, Revive. The laughter,
the drums, the music, swirling through the trees.
Echoes of magical images dancing in my dreams
inviting me to dreamland I fall asleep with ease.

(Anastasia, 2008)

No more Acid Trips!

❧

During the summer before my senior year in high school, I decided to quit smoking pot and taking acid. I did my last trip at the Oregon Country Fair when I was seventeen. I vividly remember tripping so hard that I felt like I was going to lose my mind. It didn't help that I ran into someone I knew who offered me some cocaine. I still can't believe I snorted cocaine while tripping on acid. Talk about creating chaos in your body. With the intense buzz from the cocaine mixed with the swirling hallucinations from the acid, my brain felt like it was going to melt. It felt awful. My brain overloaded and I could barely keep it together. I just sat and watched all the hippies around me make spectacles of themselves. I leaned up against a tree in the dark and waited for the intense experience to finish.

The bummer with acid is that the trip lasts for several intense hours. Night had fallen at the fair. With so much going on around me, I could only trip out and watch the crowd. At that point I realized that I had enough of that spaced-out feeling and felt tired of being burned out all the

145

time. My moods increasingly depended on whether or not I was high, and I didn't like relying on a substance to make me feel normal. What a strange concept to realize, since all I had ever wanted, as a hippie kid was to feel normal.

I wanted to take my last year of school seriously. I wanted to graduate and feel proud that I did a good job. And sure enough, I graduated. Crazy as it seems, Ken Kesey delivered the keynote address at my graduation. I had gone through my entire school experience battling the issues of being a hippie kid, only to graduate from a conservative high school and have one of the leading pioneers of the hippie movement give us our pep talk speech. Who would have imagined that?

Rebelling

❖

It seems natural that at some point during childhood or adolescence one is inclined to rebel against their family or society in some way. Even though I had stopped smoking pot and taking acid, I still hung out with my stoner friends. I just didn't partake anymore. It served as my own rebellion, I suppose. I find it funny that "normal" kids who have been raised with more conservative upbringings tend to rebel by experimenting with drugs, dressing in weird styles, and altering their lifestyle into the complete opposite of their parents'. But how does a hippie kid rebel? Being raised in a free-spirited, unsupervised, and "loose" sort of environment as we tripped through the whole hippie era alongside our parents, we essentially already lived a rebellious life. We could only go in the opposite direction. I always felt caught in the middle, being a bit too conservative to be considered a real hippie and too natural and alternative to fit in with the mainstream "straight" world.

In my experience as a hippie kid, I fought against the whole lifestyle and battled with being judged for embracing the principles of peace, love, and happiness—all the ideals and philosophies that stood for being a hippie. I struggled with the negative stereotype that portrayed hippies as lower class, rebellious misfits of society who undermined authority and smoked pot all the time (not to mention the horrible "dirty hippie" typecast).

I decided not to accept the label of hippie, but I have never felt completely comfortable fitting in with the conservative mainstream society, either. I do my best to balance the polarities of my life. I have managed to be myself. Sometimes I encounter hippies and find myself feeling outcast, not "cool" enough to be accepted, because I have a little too much mainstream conservatism in my appearance. On the flip side, I rarely find myself completely accepted by the more conservative crowd because I seem to have a sign over my head that says, " Once a hippie, always a hippie." As far as I know, other hippie kids deal with these same issues.

Some hippie kids have grown up to live a lifestyle completely opposite from how they were raised. They also have chosen to deny much of their upbringing. Perhaps they are pissed off at their parents for being so flakey and irresponsible. I also know many hippie kids who have grown up to appreciate the philosophies and the good intentions that our hippie parents lived by.

Hippies brought up their children to think for themselves, question authority, and make a difference in the world. They taught us to respect others, love our "brothers" and "sisters," and create peace wherever we go. Even though our hippie parents may have been irresponsible at times, they had good intentions and they meant well.

For each kid, the experience of being raised in those early hippie days may be different, but we all share a common bond unique from any other time in history. As we look back, we must remember that we came from a generation that actually did make a difference in the world.

Some common hippie terms and how they are used:

Mellow out, man: Don't be so uptight. Relax.

Far out: Wow, that's pretty interesting. I can relate. Very cool.

Can you dig it? (Ya dig?): Do you understand? Do you see where I'm coming from?

Peace: Used frequently as a farewell remark or a greeting in passing. Also used to control intense emotions in a confrontation. "Peace brother, calm down, mellow out."

Good Vibes: Positive feelings in the atmosphere or surroundings. Also a light happy energy put off from an individual.

Bad Vibes: Negative emotions or feelings put off from an individual who is uptight. Very negative and tense feelings in a room or in the air as a result of a bad situation.

Go with the flow: Be flexible and open to change. Release the need to be too much in control.

Right on: All right. I know what you mean. I agree with you.

Out of sight: That's great! Amazing!

Groovy: I like it. Everything is good. A feel-good term

Cool: A descriptive word, which expresses great approval. Also, maintaining control of your emotions.

Sister: Not necessarily referring to a sibling. Often a way to address a woman, especially if you don't know her name. "Hey sister, how's it going?"

Brother: A term used to address a man. *See "sister" description.

Heavy: Something intense.

Heavy duty: Something really intense. Could also be said in response to hearing bad news. "Wow, that's heavy duty, man."

Bad trip: Enduring a negative experience, either under the influence of drugs or under normal circumstances.

Good trip: A positive experience. Most commonly used to describe a fun time while tripping on LSD/acid.

Tripping: Being under the influence of a psychedelic drug such as LSD/acid. Also a term used to let someone know that they are thinking too deeply about something. "Man, you are just tripping, let it go."

Straight: A term used to describe someone who is not a hippie. Conservative. Also a judgmental term referring to a closed-minded individual.

Trippy: A way to describe something unusual. Out of the ordinary. Oddly interesting. Colorful and unique. Used also as a comeback. "That's pretty trippy!"

(Anastasia, 2009)

"Wandering"

She was just a child, bound to her mother. Wandering side-by-side—alone together. Always wondering, never knowing where their journeys would take them.

She was just a child, following her mother toward the One. Without a home, feeling lost, never staying long enough to know someone.

Her eyes saw the world through many colors and spectrums. Learning. Loving. Leaving. Heart-breaking good-byes. Tomorrows brought new friends only to be left behind again.

Her fears were set aside by hope and trust. Trusting in her mother, knowing somehow everything would be all right.

Always moving, changing, growing. Creating memories, happy and sad. Making peace within herself that she could live her life without her dad.

Learning that "home is where the heart is." Making the best of any situation. Keeping faith and knowing that this is just "how it is."

Lessons. Experiences. Life unfolding. She was just a child. Growing older, wiser, moving on and on...following her mother toward the One.

(Anastasia, 2010)

Today

❧

The hippie culture has continued to stay strong, infiltrating the third and fourth generations of hippie children. The values, beliefs, and lifestyle have become much more widely accepted and respected, perhaps because as the original hippies matured, their behaviors and values became more refined.

Present-day hippies still gather to rally for peace, oppose war, and make a difference in the world. There is now a global awareness of how important whales and all ocean life is in regards to the health of our planet, thanks to the Greenpeace organizations. Rainbow Gatherings continue to take place annually. Communes still exist and are referred to as: "intentional living communities." Dietary awareness is linked to the early hippie health food fanatics, as well as conscious eating habits of choosing to eat locally and organically. The importance of healthy living, sustainable living, recycling, thoughtful awareness and treating the earth with respect are all concepts generated from those early hippie values and ideals that sounded a bit crazy and unrealistic in the first conceptual stages. The radical ideas and unusual philosophies produced by the hippie culture did in fact make a positive impact on our society. In my lifetime I have noticed a growing awareness and common understanding that we as humans have a responsibility to care for our planet, and that our actions make a big impact… either positive or negative, depending on the choices we make and how we choose to live.

As I look back on my childhood, many feelings flow through me. For the most part I have accepted all of the unusual circumstances and experiences, realizing that they made me who I am. I appreciate and feel honored to be a part of such a unique culture, regardless of the controversies. I realize that I can't change my past, but I can change how I interpret it. So I choose to look at the difficult events and struggles of my childhood with a new perspective. By doing this I can see the lessons, rather than feel burdened with the hurt, shame, or anger.

That era was a crazy time for those who chose to partake in the lifestyle. And for those of us born into it, we each have our own experience and interpretation of "what a long strange trip it's been" (Jerry Garcia). Thank you for allowing me to share my story and perspective of the early hippie days with you all.

We are who we are.

Life is what it is.

Love it, live it, accept it!

With Love and Gratitude,

Anastasia

Made in the USA
Las Vegas, NV
15 December 2022